New Vintage

New Vintage

THE HOMEMADE HOME

BEAUTIFUL INTERIORS AND HOW-TO PROJECTS

Tahn Scoon

photographs by Anastasia Kariofyllidis

NH
NEW
HOLLAND

For Sassie

Contents

Introduction

A home filled with beautifully crafted hand and homemade pieces is a home filled with warmth and soul.

When I was growing up, my dad repaired and recycled our furniture, extensively renovated our house and built a 40-foot yacht in our front yard. My mum was a wonderful cook and also made many of our clothes, cushions and curtains. Aside from the yacht, which I'm still in awe over, all this was considered quite normal. However, along the way, subsequent generations have largely lost these everyday domestic skills—and I guess this book is a little about re-claiming them.

I've been lucky enough to meet some wonderfully generous people who have shown me how to restore vintage furniture, sew simple soft furnishings and plant a small kitchen garden. Learning (or in some cases, re-learning) these skills has been very rewarding and I hope you enjoy the process as much as I did.

Be daring enough to fill your home with the things you love; the homemade, the handmade, the well-worn and the well-loved—and boldly combine them with the clean sensibilities of the new—and you'll have a home that is truly beautiful and absolutely you. Enjoy.

A BEAUTIFUL HOME
the bare bones

Sympathetically Renovating a Character Home

If you're thinking of renovating an older home, it's a good idea to research homes of that era so that you can form an understanding of which architectural features are original to the home—and should be preserved.

The workmanship and materials used in building many older homes are superb, and hard to replicate (some of those skills are almost gone), so it's important not to tear things out until you find out what they are—they may be of great historical and cultural relevance.

Certainly remove any poorly made subsequent additions to the original home, but honour and retain the architectural features that are precious—it's these details that give the home its soul.

Adding Soul to a New Home

Conversely, you may want to add more character and depth to a new home by installing traditional architectural features such as profiled cornices and skirtings, and tongue and groove panelling. Just keep in mind that most new builds are fairly clean in their design and any additions need to be too. Anything too ornate won't blend comfortably with the original design.

Another way to add soul to a new home is to use salvaged materials, such as recycled timber for flooring and cabinetry. It's especially lovely when it comes with its own history; for example, it may have been salvaged from a local wharf or town hall.

Life-sized statues, affectionately known as Isabella and Francine, recline around the 3.3 metre deep plunge pool, which sits within the original saw-tooth external factory walls of this contemporary home.

Cleaning

The first step to creating a gorgeous home is to thoroughly clean it. In most cases, you don't need much more than hot, soapy water (generally, if water's too hot to touch; it's too hot for germs). If there's something particularly nasty to deal with, try the recipe for disinfectant on page 38.

If you have just bought an older home, hire a professional house cleaning company to also clean the exterior walls and inside the roof, which may be filled with years' worth of dust, droppings and worse.

Another cleansing thing to do is open every door and window to let the sun and fresh air flow in. In a practical sense, this helps to rid the house of stale air, dust mites and other undesirables—and in a more emotive sense, it cleanses the home of 'old energy' (I also like to play classical music loudly to fill the new space with beautiful sound).

Walls

Next, look at what you need to do to improve the home. Walls are often the easiest component to deal with. More often than not they can be freshened up with a simple coat of paint and this is usually a job you can easily do yourself (the only exceptions may be if the walls are very high or the substrate very difficult).

As for paint colours, my preferred method is to use soft whites and creams to freshen and open up a home—and then I like to add colour via wallpaper, art and furnishings as the home evolves. If I do use stronger colours on the walls, I tend to select dramatic deep charcoals and taupes and contrast them with lighter accessories.

Use low VOC (volatile organic compound) paints to protect your health and the environment, and paint with windows and doors open to ensure good ventilation. You may even want to go one step further and paint with a traditional paint, such as milk paint, which contains no VOCs (and therefore no harmful and unpleasant smells).

Windows and Doors

The paint on timber doors and around window frames in older homes is usually oil-based enamel. Oil-based enamels are one of the most toxic paints on the market (which is why most companies are now producing water-based enamels instead) and they are a lot harder to sand back than wall paint. However, you don't have to get it all off; as long as you get the gloss off, it will be fine to re-paint. If you'd like to re-paint with a water-based enamel, use an all-purpose acrylic primer first.

Good painting is all in the preparation; so don't skimp on the sanding no matter how tedious. Also, keep in mind that most paints manufactured before 1970 contained lead—so before sanding anything in an older house, buy a lead-testing kit (very cheap and easy to use, and available at big hardware stores) and check for lead first.

Aluminium windows and doorframes can be a little trickier to beautify. If you have the money, add character to the home by replacing them with beautiful salvaged pieces. I've seen internal bedroom doors replaced with vintage 'Powder Room' doors salvaged from a ladies' restroom and aluminium sliding doors replaced with old red, timber shop doors—it looks fabulous.

However, if your budget doesn't allow for replacements, aluminium frames can be painted out in the same colour as the architraves so they become less obvious. White frames on white architraves and walls work particularly well. Aluminium needs to be prepared properly before painting. You'll need to rough the frames back with a scouring pad and then apply an adhesive primer.

Floors

When it comes to flooring, it's often most desirable to work with what you have. If you're lucky enough to rip up old carpet to reveal hardwood floorboards—simply have them sanded, re-stained (if needed) and sealed. Though you can save a little money by hiring a sander and sanding back the floors yourself, it's often not worth the risk of damaging the timber—hardwood is precious and can only be sanded so many times.

Freshly stained and raw floorboards need to be sealed for durability. Avoid solvent-based polyurethane coatings as most are extremely toxic (and banned in parts of Europe and the US) and opt for non-toxic water-based polyurethane coatings instead. Water-based coatings also tend to look more natural and less shiny or 'plastic'. Seek out companies that specialise in healthier, eco-friendly finishes.

Alternatively, seal floors with an eco-friendly hard wax oil. Though this is a slightly more expensive option, the finish is absolutely divine as the hard wax oil penetrates and treats the timber, bringing out all of its

natural beauty and patina. The finish is soft and tactile with a 'hand-done' quality to it. It's completely non-toxic, 100 per cent natural and sourced from renewable resources.

Other options are to apply tung oil or a beeswax polish. However, Tung Oil is petroleum-based and contains harmful chemicals (it can be particularly bothersome for those with asthma), and a beeswax polish won't permanently seal the floors, so they'll need to be re-done very regularly.

If you have softwood floors, such as pine, you may want to disguise the yellowness of the timber. You can do this by applying a deep, cool-brown timber stain to create darker floors—or you might like to try a white wood-wash for a fresh Scandinavian style. (Just keep in mind that wood-washes soak into the timber, so once they're on, they're quite hard to get off again.)

If you have dated ceramic tiles, consider ripping them up and polishing the concrete substrate for a more industrial look. Alternatively, if tiles are in good condition, you could save on the cost of having them ripped up by laying new tiles or floating a timber floor directly over the existing tiles.

If you are laying new floors, keep in mind your most eco-friendly options are bamboo, cork, recycled and forest-friendly timbers and natural fibres such as sisal and jute.

Preparing a Bathroom

- To affordably update a bathroom, paint, rather than tile, bathroom walls: it will save you a fortune. Use a satin finish acrylic as it will handle moisture and discourage mould growth (if mould is already a problem, clean first with a diluted clove oil solution—mix one teaspoon of clove oil with one litre of water into a spray bottle, spray on and leave for a few hours before washing off—then add a couple of drops of mould killer to your paint to prevent regrowth).

- Revamp old tiles by replacing damaged, discoloured grout. This is fairly easy—carefully remove the old grout with a toothed carbide grit-edge cutting blade, vacuum away the dust, then wash with warm water and vinegar. Apply the new grout, leave to set and then seal.

- Update an old toilet by simply replacing the toilet seat. In most cases the seat will be a standard size and it'll be an easy do-it-yourself project—however, some older toilets won't fit today's standard-sized seats, so check first by measuring the distance between the two back screws which attach the toilet seat to the toilet bowl and the width and length of the bowl.

- Convert an old single flush toilet into a dual flush toilet by buying a simple water-saving device, which you can install yourself in just a few minutes—miles cheaper than replacing the whole toilet.

- Instead of going to the expense of replacing or re-enamelling a chipped tub or vanity, apply a coat of epoxy enamel to achieve a smooth, fresh finish.

- If you can't afford top-end designer taps, buy the cheaper versions available at hardware stores. If you keep to the simpler styles, you won't even be able to tell the difference.

- A new shower screen will instantly freshen a tired bathroom and will make it appear larger. Again, buy from one of the larger hardware stores to get a good price. If you have some do-it-yourself experience, you may even be able to save on the installation fee. Alternatively, the most affordable option of all is a fresh, white shower curtain.

Painting rather than tiling bathroom walls will save a
fortune. A fresh white shower curtain only costs a few
dollars but instantly updates an older bathroom.

bathrooms and kitchens can be very costly to renovate. As much as we'd all love to have access to an unlimited budget—more often than not, this isn't the case.

However, don't let the lack of money deter you—there are a number of ways to affordably update these rooms.

Preparing a Kitchen

- The best way of affordably updating a kitchen is to leave the internal cabinetry intact and just revamp or replace the doors, hardware and bench tops.
- Outdated laminate cupboard doors can be painted—the trick is to use a specialised primer and then apply the paint with small mohair rollers so as to not leave brush marks. However, the result isn't wonderful so a better option is to replace the doors. If you're lucky enough to have standard door sizes, simply unscrew the old doors and replace with the new, which can be bought from the likes of IKEA.
- Replace old, unattractive cupboard knobs and handles with new ones. Hardware stores sell handles for under $10. To save you from having to fill old holes and re-drill new ones, take one of your old handles with you when you go shopping so that you can match up the size.
- If you're lucky enough to have removable, laminate bench tops you may be able to update them very affordably. Check to see whether the bench tops are secured by screws running up through the cabinets. If they are, they should be easy to un-screw and replace.
- Consider using pressed tin metal panels rather than engineered stone or tiles for the splashback. It's more affordable and easier to install and adds an industrial edge. Alternatively, seek out salvaged tiles for a cheaper, and sometimes more interesting, option.
- Source a large second-hand butcher's block to use in lieu of an island bench. Revamp with a dark stain or a coat of paint, and add a linen skirt instead of cupboard doors.

Opposite: When Anastasia and her husband Jason moved into their 1950s brick cavity home the kitchen was an eyesore. To keep costs down, they decided to renovate themselves. Freestanding pieces were sourced, mainly bought at sales, and used in lieu of built-in cabinetry. The commercial stainless steel sink was also bought as a loose piece and a linen cloth curtain was added to hide contents and soften the look of the steel. The splashbacks are pressed metal panels, which have been powder-coated in grey. The overall effect is a very cool collaboration of French provincial and industrial styles. The really amazing thing is how little this kitchen cost—well under $5000 (excluding appliances).

Re-decorating for Renters

When you're renting, you may not think it's worth doing too much as it's not your house—however, keep in mind, it is your home. I've had some lovely private rental situations where the landlords/ladies did let me do little alterations around the home (such as dig a garden or paint the internal walls) and they were charming about it. However, some owners and real estate agents are more difficult, so always seek permission in writing first if you want to make any substantial changes.

Whether you are allowed to make any substantial or structural changes or not, you can certainly make the following superficial changes (just remember to have everything back to how it was when you leave).

- Use reversible laminate wall panels from IKEA to hide an ugly splashback. The panels can be cut to size, they're easy to install and don't leave any marks when you take them down.
- Update cupboard doors by replacing the handles; just remember to keep the old ones so you can pop them back on when you move out.
- Replace tired, plain light shades with more interesting ones. Keep in mind you can only do this with simple D.I.Y. batten-fixed shades. To check whether you have a D.I.Y. batten-fixed shade, try to unscrew it. If it easily unscrews with no exposed wiring, it's fine to remove and replace with a new shade. However, if this isn't the case and the shade doesn't easily unscrew, you will have to call in an electrician.
- Pack away any outdated curtains and replace with simple and affordable calico or muslin curtains. Muslin is lovely and light and makes a great sheer curtain (see How-to Simple Sheer Curtain) and calico is a more affordable alternative to linen for windows that need more coverage (see How-to Linen Curtain).
- If you have unattractive overhead cupboard doors, try removing them to create open shelving instead. You may find the cupboard carcases are a plain white and much more appealing to live with.
- Use wall decals to decorate a nursery or children's room. (I think they can look a little cheap in other rooms, but the designer options for children's spaces are adorable.)
- If you'd love a linen-upholstered bedhead (see How-to) but don't want to leave holes in the wall, make a much taller bedhead that rests directly on the ground—easy to take with you and no patching up of walls.
- If you have a lot of art, consider mounting a picture rail, professional tracking system, or shelf, which will leave you with fewer holes to repair when you leave. Alternatively, attach foam pads to the backs of large pieces and gently lean them against the wall.

Creating a Comfortable Home

For a home to be inviting to visitors and gorgeous to live in, it needs to be comfortable. Homes that are too hot or too cold are not comfortable—and we simply don't enjoy being in them—so it's important to deal with any cooling and heating issues.

Keeping Your Home Cool

The most effective way to keep your home cool is to insulate it adequately. You can save up to 45 per cent on energy used for cooling by adding roof and ceiling insulation, and a further 20 per cent by insulating the walls. The addition of a roof ventilation system, such as a whirly-bird, will expel any hot air that does accumulate.

Cross ventilation is also important. Track the movement of breezes through your home and determine if there are any obstructions. Enclosed verandas may be opened up, solid garden walls replaced with lattice, or windows added to allow the breeze through. In the absence of breezes, personal and ceiling fans can be used to create air movement and assist ventilation. Ceiling fans in particular are incredibly energy efficient and can cut the need for air-conditioning by more than half.

Air-conditioners are cost intensive, both financially and environmentally, and it is best to use them efficiently. Avoid installing air-conditioners in high indoor-outdoor traffic zones; instead place in the one or two rooms that will benefit the most and keep windows and doors closed while running.

Windows can be the greatest source of unwanted heat gain into a home. To prevent the penetration of this heat, glass must be protected. Whilst heavy curtains and close-fitting blinds certainly offer good relief, the most effective means is by shading externally. Direct sun can radiate as much energy as a single-bar heater. Shading can block up to 90 per cent of this heat. External shading options include pergolas, shutters, eaves, verandas and planting. Clever planting is fabulous because it adds good looks to your home as well. Trees with high canopies will block the high summer sun on the northern aspect, but allow the lower winter sun through. Alternatively, deciduous trees could be used for the same purpose. On the east and west, lower, thicker trees and shrubs will stop the low angled sun from penetrating. Again, deciduous varieties could be used if winter sun was desired.

If external shading devices are not an option due to lack of access, or the unwillingness to block a view, treated glass (such as toned, or low-E) or the use of a reflective coating will help to keep radiant heat out.

The exterior colour of your home should be light to reflect the heat and keep the temperature down inside. Up to one-third of all unwanted heat comes in through the roof, so it is particularly important to avoid a dark coloured roof. Light colours make us feel cooler psychologically and are physically cooler to touch. Pavers, therefore, need to be a light colour. However, light-coloured pavers outside north-facing windows may reflect unwanted glare into the home, so try planting a good ground cover instead.

Keeping Your Home Warm

Insulation works both ways, so all the suggestions for cooling, also work for heating. In addition, use a feather to track down the source of any draughts and fill any cracks or gaps in skirting boards, walls and joins with filler. Place fabric snakes under doorways, lay thick rugs on bare floors and close up unused milk and mail chutes.

As with cooling, the right window treatments are very important. To keep heat in use thick, tight-fitting curtains and add pelmets—blinds and timber venetians won't keep the heat in very effectively. Whilst in summer it's wise to keep the curtains closed during the day to keep the heat out, in winter it's more desirable to leave the curtains open to allow the heat in (but remember to close them once the sun goes down to retain the warmth).

Traditional fireplaces are romantic, but unfortunately not that great for the environment or our health (they can produce carbon monoxide, among other pollutants). They're also notoriously inefficient as around 85 per cent of the heat escapes up the chimney. However, there are now new contemporary slow-combustion fireplaces on the market, which heat more efficiently with less pollution.

If you have high ceilings, you may find a lot of your heat sits up near the ceiling; install a ceiling fan to help distribute it more evenly around the room.

Relaxed elegance in shades of grey. Furnishings
from Les Salles.

DECADENT ROOMS
a room-by-room guide

Healthy Rooms

Formaldehyde is one of the most common indoor pollutants. It is a chemical used widely in many building materials, paints and permanent press fabrics. Unfortunately, formaldehyde 'off gasses' and even at fairly low levels can cause eye, ear and throat irritation and breathing difficulties in some people.

Keep your home healthy as well as beautiful with the following tips.

Furniture

Reduce your family's exposure to formaldehyde by avoiding furniture made with pressed wood products such as fibreboard (MDF), particleboard and plywood—all of which use formaldehyde as a binding agent. Instead opt for eco-furniture constructed from plantation or recycled timbers, or timber alternatives, such as bamboo.

If you have existing MDF furniture, seal any exposed ends with a coat of milk paint or shellac. Alternatively, try EO particleboard, which has all the practicality of other particleboards but emits much lower levels of formaldehyde.

Another good option is vintage furniture: it's either finished with natural shellac and beeswax or it's already 'off-gassed' years ago.

Paint

Most commercial paints on the market contain all sorts of harmful chemicals know as VOCs (volatile organic compounds). The worst offenders are oil-based enamels, which should be avoided where possible (up to 60 per cent VOCs). Water-based paints have much lower levels of VOCs but care should still be taken when painting. Never let anyone, particularly a child, sleep in a freshly painted room—air it out thoroughly until all the 'new paint' smell has gone.

An even better option is to avoid the smell, and therefore the chemicals, by using natural paints containing no VOCs.

Fabrics

When buying bed linen, choose natural fibres as they work in harmony with the body; regulating temperature and allowing skin to breath. The best choices are linen, wool, hemp and organic cotton. (Conventional cotton growers use staggering amounts of pesticides.).

Similarly, select mattresses made with as many natural fibres as possible—and avoid synthetic foam mattresses as they emit formaldehyde and other chemicals. Also avoid permanent press and stain-protected fabrics for drapery and upholstery for similar reasons. Opt for natural linens and cottons instead: they will stain more easily but you can counteract that a little by choosing pre-shrunk washable fabrics, which are easy to clean. Protect upholstered furniture with washable slipcovers.

Floors

Carpet can be wonderfully comforting in the bedroom—however, synthetic carpets contain all sorts of chemical nasties, so choose pure wool with natural jute backing and have it tacked into place instead of glued.

For those with asthma or other allergies, it is best to avoid carpet all together as it harbours dust mites, which can trigger attacks. Timber, bamboo or linoleum (made from linseed) floors are the healthiest and most environmentally friendly—but be mindful of what glues and finishes are used.

If you choose timber floors, avoid harsh chemical sealers and stains; instead, seek out natural oils, waxes and plant-based floor vanishes.

Plants

It's well known that plants convert carbon dioxide to oxygen, but less well known that they also absorb and store pollutants—therefore adding plants to the bedroom is a simple, natural way to instantly improve air quality.

The best plants are those with broad leafs and strong root systems, as they are better able to absorb more pollutants. Studies carried out at NASA named the peace lily and tropical palms as being the most effective. The University of Technology in Sydney backed this up when they discovered that kentia palms, placed in an enclosed room, eliminated benzene, a known carcinogen, by 90 per cent after only 24 hours.

The Green Clean

The smell of Sunlight Soap (a mild household cleaning soap) always reminds me of my great nana's house. It was always so beautiful and clean but in a fresh, natural way. Chemicals were very rarely used—usually just good old-fashioned soap, sunlight and water.

For *New Vintage*-style cleaning, stock up on:

Pure soap (a mild household cleaning soap)
White vinegar
Baking soda
Eucalyptus oil
Tea Tree oil
Lemons
Borax

All-Purpose Surface Spray

To make your own all-purpose surface spray to clean benches, mirrors, windows, toilet seats and other surfaces, mix the following ingredients into a spray bottle.

¾ cup of white vinegar
¼ cup of water
20 drops of Eucalyptus oil

All-Purpose Surface Cream

This is a slightly more abrasive surface cleaner, which is particularly good on chrome and porcelain surfaces. Simply mix the baking soda and water together to form a paste, which you rub on and wipe off. It'll leave a lovely shine.

4 tablespoons of baking soda
4 tablespoons of warm water

Floor Cleaner

I love this recipe for cleaning floors. When you add the baking soda to the vinegar, it fizzes up, which is somehow very satisfying.

A bucket of hot water
½ cup of vinegar
¼ cup of baking soda
A few drops of Tea Tree oil

Disinfectant

This is a more eco-friendly disinfectant for regular household use. Borax is a natural mineral and therefore not harmful to the environment—however, it's not so gentle on the skin, so wear gloves and keep away from children.

¼ cup of borax
¼ cup of vinegar
Juice of ½ a lemon
Hot water

Dishwashing Powder

Commercial dishwashing powder is one of the most toxic chemicals found in the home. Use less of it by substituting half of the powder for baking soda, and using white vinegar in the rinse cycle.

Cleaning Windows

Windows come up beautifully if you wash them with hot, soapy water and then rinse them with clean hot water and vinegar.

For Good Measure

Here are some standard measurements, which may come in handy.

Furniture and Cabinetry

- Dining Table—Average width, 90 centimetres (36 inches). You need about 60 centimetres (24 inches) in length for each diner and at least 80 centimetres (32 inches) of space between the table and wall to allow for chairs to be pulled out.

- Kitchen and Island Benches—Kitchen benches are generally 90 centimetres (36 inches) high; however, you may want to go higher if you're taller. Island benches are usually the same height, but go lower if you bake/cook a lot, as 80 centimetres (32 inches) is a better height for kneading, chopping and mixing. Barstools need to be 30 centimetres (12 inches) lower than the counter.

- Sofas—The average three-seat sofa is 200–230 x 90 centimetres (80–92 x 36 inches) deep; the average two-seat, 180–190 x 90 centimetres (72–76 x 36 inches) deep; and a single seat, 90–100 x 90 centimetres (36–40 x 36 inches) deep. The coffee table should be around the same height as the sofa and placed around 50 centimetres (20 inches) away.

- Beds—A king size bed is 183 x 203 centimetres (73 x 81 inches); queen 153 x 203 centimetres (61 x 81 inches); double 137 x 187 centimetres (55 x 75 inches); king single 106 x 203 centimetres (42.5 x 81 inches) and a single 92 x 187 centimetres (37 x 75 inches). Bedside tables should be the same height as the top of the mattress and lamps no higher than the top of the bedhead.

Distances and Heights

- The television should be at approximately three times the screen width away from viewers.
- A chandelier should be hung at least 75 centimetres (30 inches) off the table.
- The average ceiling height is 2.4 metres (7 feet 10.5 inches), but 2.7 metre-high (8 feet 10.3 inches) ceilings create a greater sense of opulence.
- The average door height is 2.1 metres (6 feet 10.7 inches), but in a new build, go higher to create an illusion of more space.
- When placing furniture, walkways need to be at least 1 metre (3 feet 3.37 inches) wide.
- A bedroom needs to be at least 5 x 5 metres (16 feet 4.85 inches) to accommodate a king size bed.
- A kitchen needs to be at least 2.4 x 3.5 metres (7 feet 10.5 inches x 11 feet 5.8 inches) to comfortably accommodate an island bench.

The Bathroom

- A freestanding bath makes the biggest statement. The old claw-foot baths are still the best as they were built to last (which is why you still see them standing around in paddocks!). If you're lucky enough to find one, have it re-enamelled inside and paint the outside a deep charcoal shade.

- Select lighting that you would more commonly find in other rooms; a chandelier adds instant decadence, whilst lamp-style wall sconces create a luxury hotel ambience.

- Mount wall sconces at eye-height on either side of the mirror for the most flattering light (overhead light will cast shadows on your face, highlighting wrinkles and worse!).

- Natural light is the most beautiful of all in a bathroom—if you don't have enough, consider adding a skylight or replacing a small window with a bigger window. If, on the other hand, you have too much natural light, soften with curtains and paint or tile the walls in a darker, moodier shade.

- Freestanding furniture creates an opulent but relaxed feel. Vintage dressers can be used in place of fitted cabinetry, just ensure all timber pieces are painted or sealed.

- Select 'real' finishes and materials, such as sealed timber, travertine and river stones wherever possible. (Timber requires some maintenance, as it needs to be re-sealed now and then, but it brings so much warmth and character to the room, it's worth it.)

- Outdoor fabric is designed to tolerate moisture and will perform well in a bathroom. It can be used for roman blinds, curtains or even shower curtains. Add a burst of colour with a bright French stripe.

- An oversized mirror will look fabulous in any sized bathroom and will double the sense of space in a small bathroom.

- Wallpaper will add instant luxe. Just remember to choose a vinyl paper, ensure the room has adequate ventilation (or the paper will eventually lift) and select a wall well away from the shower.

- Select unusual cabinet handles such as crystal-style knobs or a mismatched collection of vintage handles.

- If space permits, add a comfortable chair, for sitting and chatting to bathers. If your bathroom is too steamy for an upholstered chair, sew a terry-towelling slipcover for a timber chair. If possible, re-locate the toilet to a separate room—at the very least, hide it with a concealed cistern and a simple partition (and decorate with a striking wallpaper).

A larger, well-ventilated bathroom can cope with a comfy upholstered chair.

Just because it's often a small, practical space there's no need for it to be overly utilitarian— add some bling and bring on the bliss.

A sheer black curtain, opulent light fittings and high-gloss freestanding drawers give this bathroom a decadent 'dressing room' quality.

Traditional fixtures and finishes add warmth
to a new bathroom.

Fresh oysters w/...

Chermoula Lamb Cutlets w/
yoghurt & mint

Semi-dried
vine tomato
Pastries w/
Caramelised onion
+ basil

Asparagus,
Gruyere &
Prosciutto Tarts

Roast Carrot &
Beetroot Salad
w/ garlic & thyme

Fattoush
Salad

Chocolate
mud cup
cakes w/
Strawberries

Yum!

The Kitchen

- Update a plain kitchen instantly by adding an incredible chandelier or row of vintage industrial lights. For a more organic feel, you could also try to make your own pendants from woven lobster pots or bamboo garden cloches.
- Choose timeless materials and finishes such as timber, stone or steel for cabinetry and bench tops—soften with natural fabrics such as cotton and linen. A relaxed roman blind, in cotton or linen, works particularly well in the kitchen.
- Avoid installing an overtly contemporary kitchen into an older home; it will look horribly dated in ten years (think of how many times you've walked into a home and thought, '80s kitchen' or '90s kitchen'). Select traditional finishes and classic designs.
- Transform tired, old kitchen stools by re-covering the seats in a striped linen fabric—or for a more easy-care option, a patterned oilcloth. Re-paint the frame in a high-gloss finish.
- Add more character to plain cabinetry doors by including moulded panels. Simply remove the doors and lightly sand before attaching the panels, then re-paint and re-hang.
- Wallpaper can add movement and colour to an otherwise neutral kitchen. Be bold by papering the entire kitchen, or paper behind glass-fronted cabinets for a more subtle impact. Choose a washable vinyl design.

Opposite: Eclectic industrial pieces give this kitchen its edge. Blackboard paint personalises the space and the wall is used as a message and menu board.

A simple white kitchen is enhanced by luxury touches such as a chandelier, gilded mirror and crystal-style cabinet knobs.

Nikki's Cottage: Rather impressively, my cousin Nikki built her unique kitchen bench herself out of Hebel brick. It's very strong but can be cut with just a handsaw, which makes it very easy to shape. To create a more rustic effect, Nikki splashed the leftover Hebel glue all over the bench and then smashed it until she got the look she wanted. Old cedar sleepers were incorporated into the design and then the entire bench was sealed with a clear resin.

Eating well is one of life's greatest joys; and dining rooms, even in an open-plan design, should be comfortable and inviting.

The Dining Room

- If you entertain a lot, a big, comfortable table is paramount. Whether it's a beautiful old antique or a 'found' piece, if it's big and well set it'll look fabulous. (As a rough guide, each diner will need 60 centimetres (24 inches) to sit comfortably, and you'll need to have the table at least 80 centimetres (32 inches) away from the wall so chairs can be pulled in and out.)
- If space is tight, consider bench seating along one wall (which can also double as storage).
- Create your own 'harlequin' set of vintage chairs for next to nothing (one-off chairs are miles cheaper than sets and can be easily sourced at antique stores, charity shops and garage sales). Keep the seats at similar heights to tie the chairs together.
- If you're purchasing new chairs, stick to classic designs such as the Thornet, Windsor or Bentwood—these timeless designs won't date and will retain their value. Whichever chair you choose, keep in mind it needs to be comfortable—add cushions if you need to.
- In an open-plan home, a large area rug can be used to define the dining space. The rug should be big enough so that chairs can be pulled back without slipping off.
- Chandeliers and pendants need to sit at least 75 centimetres (30 inches) above the table. To calculate how big a chandelier should be in relation to your table; subtract 30 centimetres (15 inches) from the width of the table.
- Antique embroidered lace tablecloths are often too small or stained in spots—cut out the good sections and sew together to create one gorgeous large tablecloth.

Opposite: Matthew Cheyne's 'Penelope' looks down over the large contemporary dining table, which has been teamed with 1950s brushed metal French chairs from Industrial Revolution.

The Living Room

There are more options available than simply teaming a modular sofa with MDF cabinetry, think creatively and don't be afraid to be a little eclectic.

- The sofa is the big piece in the living room and it needs to be comfortable, so I never go vintage here unless I can afford to have it fully reupholstered. In most cases, it's best to invest in a new sofa and make it a good one. Look for a steel base, hardwood frame and foam-wrapped feather cushioning. A decent sofa is a big ticket item, but worth it.

- 'Found' furniture is perfect in the living room. Revamp timber pieces to use as sideboards and tables—and re-upholster vintage chairs in 'look-at-me' fabrics to create a personalised and eclectic space.

- If you require additional seating, consider making up some floor cushions—especially great for movie nights and children. Remember to pre-shrink the fabric first for easy washing (see page 101).

- Storage is all-important in living areas, especially for families, so make sure you have an adequate amount. There's two ways to go here; vintage freestanding pieces to make a statement, or built-in cabinetry designed to fade into the background.

- With the exception of the odd beautifully framed vintage print—always hang originals, even if they're just your child's drawing (which can look absolutely fantastic when hung properly). If you're hanging a group of works of different sizes, line them up at the bottom to create a sense of order.

- One big rug is always better than many small rugs. To define the living area in an open-plan home, place a large area rug under the coffee table and sofa (preferably, all four legs of the sofa should be on the rug; however, you can get away with just the front two).

Opposite: Custom cabinetry is painted in the wall colour to allow it to sit comfortably in the room. The black feature wallpaper is 'Manaus' wallpaper by Nina Campbell.

A former school cupboard has been given a new lease of

A Note on Storage

If you opt for custom built-in cabinetry, use the opportunity to design the perfect storage for your household. Consider including pullout toy bins for toddlers, school bag cupboards for older children or perhaps a drinks cabinet for yourself. The more organised your home, the more relaxed you'll feel (particularly after you've installed that drinks cabinet).

Deep diamond-buttoned fabric ottomans look great in the living room and can be fitted with hinged lids to store magazines and books—as can a purpose-built window seat. (I find being able to tidy up quickly helps preserve my sanity.)

And don't forget the best storage tip of all—get rid of anything you don't use or need—the less you have to put away, the better!

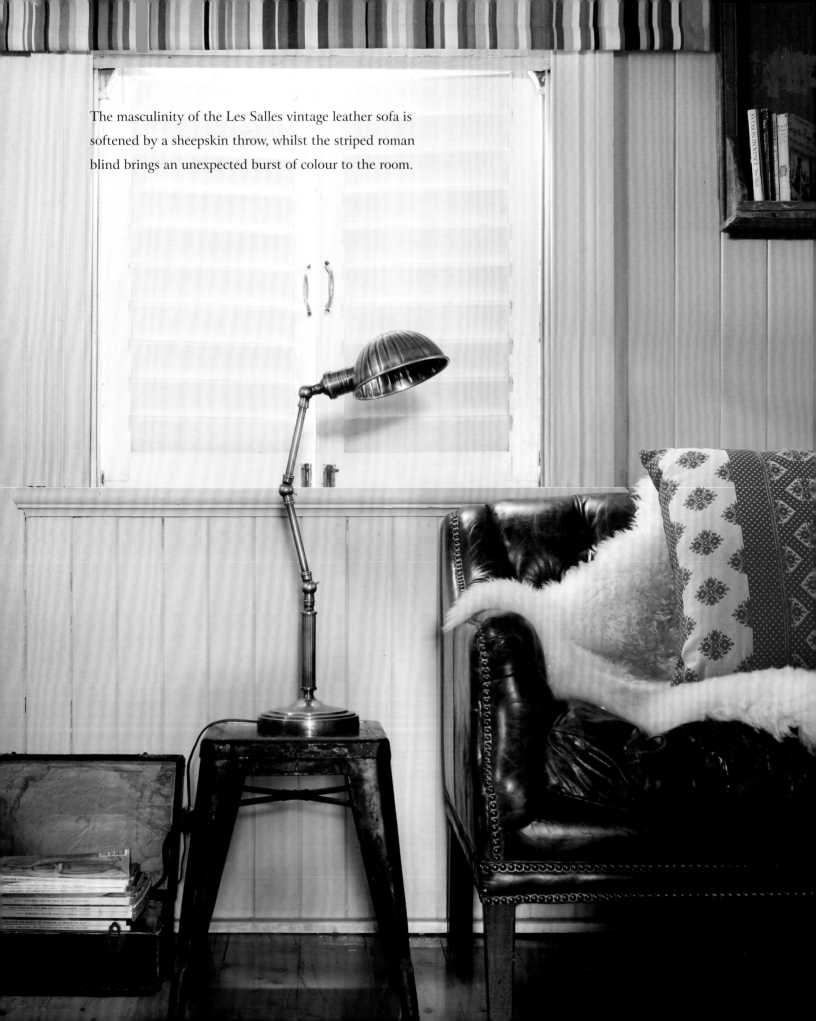

The masculinity of the Les Salles vintage leather sofa is softened by a sheepskin throw, whilst the striped roman blind brings an unexpected burst of colour to the room.

The Bedroom

- The bed is the centrepiece of the decadent bedroom and should be big and sensual with beautiful linen. Some people have a tendency to over-decorate beds with pillows. Don't. Two European, two standard and one feature cushion are ample.

- Whether to buy an ensemble or slat bed is a personal choice; slat beds work well in humid climates as they allow more air to circulate, but ensembles somehow feel more luxurious. If you do choose an ensemble, cover the base with a bespoke tailored linen bed skirt.

- Unusual bedside choices, such as metal tables, look striking, but be prepared to be seriously tidy—bedsides with drawers are much more practical. As a general rule of thumb, bedside tables should be the same height as the top of the mattress and lamps no higher than the top of the headboard.

- Wallpaper lends a sense of glamour and can be used on all walls, as a feature wall, or even on the bedhead. If you choose to do only one feature wall, make it the wall behind your bed—and paint the remaining walls in the paper's background colour.

- Install double rods (or tracks) so that you can indulge in two sets of curtains; one heavier and lined with block-out to keep out the early morning light, and one sheer to allow a softer version of the daylight in without losing privacy.

- We very rarely need strong overhead lighting in the bedroom; opt for soft, indirect light from low-wattage lamps and wall sconces instead. Have two-way switches installed, with one switch next to the bed, so you don't have to get up to turn off the lights (and also ask for all lights to be fitted with dimmers).

- As the bedroom is a space where you are likely to be barefooted, think about indulging in fine floor treatments. The tactile pleasure of plush wool carpet, or thick sheepskin rugs thrown over smooth bare floors is hard to resist.

The owner of this bedroom wanted to introduce wallpaper but didn't want to paper over the original tongue and groove walls—so wallpapered the bedhead instead (in 'Edo' by Osbourne and Little). If you'd like to try something similar at home, have an EO particleboard cut to size and cover with a (washable) vinyl wallpaper.

As the most private and sensual room of the house, the bedroom deserves to be deliciously decorated. Industrial-style lamps and charcoal accents add an edge to this predominantly taupe and white bedroom.

Children's Rooms

- There's something about patchwork that just works so well in a child's room. Try sourcing vintage handkerchiefs and sewing them together to create a small sheer curtain; buy wallpaper samples and attach them, patchwork-style, above the bed. You can sometimes find sample books of vintage wallpaper online. You can tear out the pages and attach them to the wall with glue, Blu-Tack or pins (if kids can't reach the pins); or make a patchwork throw out of your child's outgrown clothes.

- Stripes also work beautifully; they never date and it'll take many years for your child to outgrow them. Use masking tape (and a steady hand) to paint stripes onto a dresser; hang thickly striped wallpaper; invest in a striped wool rug; or make up striped canvas slipcovers for chairs and ottomans.

- Avoid MDF furniture where possible. Revamp solid timber pieces instead. However, always make sure any pre-loved nursery furniture complies with current safety standards.

- If you're painting the walls white, it's a good idea to choose a soft off-white rather than a stark pure white, which sometimes looks too clinical for a child's room.

- Install cotton or linen curtains, or roman blinds lined with blockout fabric to encourage longer sleep-ins and afternoon naps. Plain roman blinds can be beautifully embellished and personalised by embroidery, appliqué or a trim. Be aware of safety issues with blinds and curtains; children can get entangled in the cords.

- Customise a pendant drum light by carefully cutting away the original fabric and replacing with strips of ribbon. Tie or glue the strips on to the top frame and allow them to flutter down past the bottom frame. Always ensure the frame is large enough to keep the ribbon a safe distance away from the globe—and never fully enclose the globe, always leave the top and bottom open.

- Most importantly, add pieces that mean something to your child, whether it's a vintage tricycle, which has been passed down through the generations or a favourite tutu from a ballet concert—show your child that you love who they are.

Opposite: Well-lived and well-loved pieces make a child's
room precious. The doll's pram in this little girl's room
was originally owned by her grandmother.

A vintage metal child's chair and Kewpie doll.

Children are innately curious and imaginative and they'll really appreciate an eclectic, creative space to call their own.

Good Lighting

During the day a home needs plenty of good natural light. If your home doesn't have enough, consider installing a skylight, replacing solid internal doors with glass-panelled doors or replacing windows with French doors.

On the other hand, some homes can have too much natural light—in this case, soften the light with sheer muslin or linen curtains, or roman blinds and consider planting or other external shading.

To light the house at night, I prefer one stunning pendant rather than rows of downlights. If one pendant doesn't give enough light, support it with table and floor lamps. Layering light in this way creates a lovely ambience.

The queen of all pendant lighting is the chandelier; if you're lucky to find a genuine antique piece, remember to have the wiring checked by an electrician (if it's too expensive to have re-wired, use drip-less candles instead of bulbs).

When entertaining, or just relaxing, there's nothing quite like the soft, ethereal beauty of candlelight. However, traditional paraffin wax candles produce a black soot that contains at least two known carcinogenic toxins, so it's much more beneficial to seek out healthy soy oil candles instead.

A Note on Hanging Pendants and Chandeliers

Pendants and chandeliers need high enough ceilings so that you can freely walk under them with plenty of room to spare. The exception is over a table or kitchen bench and in this instance the bottom of the pendant should be at least 75 centimetres (30 inches) above the table or bench top if your ceilings are 2.4 metres (7 feet 10.5 inches), proportionally higher if your ceilings are higher

Always have pendants and chandeliers installed by a qualified electrician.

As a blend of black and white, grey is a true neutral and can project a sense of clarity and calm.

THE PAINTBOX
how to work with colour

Colour inspiration can come from anywhere. A brightly striped red and white umbrella at the beach, pale green and pink macaroons at a French patisserie or the soft velvety creams of a ragdoll kitten can all inspire new schemes.

Fashion magazines are often better for colour inspiration than interior magazines, as you seem to find more daring colour combinations. Tear out pictures of the colours that attract you the most, take photos of the places you love—sooner or later you'll discover which colours you'll want to live with in your home.

The trick to decorating with white is to layer and use different textures. In this bedroom the linen is heavily embossed and the walls are panelled. White always works beautifully with natural materials such as timber—in this instance, the darkly stained pine floors.

Cool

Neutral

Warm

The Right White

With hundreds of shades available, choosing which white paint to work with can be tricky—but much easier if you have a basic understanding of how they are categorised. Broadly speaking, whites fall into three groups: neutral, cool and warm.

Neutral Whites

These are the pure whites—the 'white-whites'. A pure white will be too harsh for most home interior applications (with the exception of a very contemporary space) and better suited to art galleries and other commercial buildings. The whites in most homes are, in fact, off-whites.

Cool Whites

Cool whites are technically off-whites as they have undertones of blue, green, grey or black.

Cool whites are crisp, fresh and very contemporary and work well with contemporary architecture—the cool hues echoed in man-made materials such as stainless steel and glass.

The cool tints are literally cooling, making these shades perfect for homes that receive too much sun. In this instance, it's best to choose a deeper shade of cool white to help soften any potential glare.

Warm Whites

Warm, creamy whites, are also technically off-whites as they have undertones of red, brown or yellow.

Warm whites have a traditional feel to them and suit older-style homes perfectly. They inject warmth and intimacy into a room and work well with natural textures like timber.

Though warm whites will literally warm up a sun-deprived home—choose the lightest shades possible to add more light.

Painting Tips for White Paint

White looks best when it's layered and there's a simple way to do this—use the same white on walls, skirtings and ceilings, but in different gloss levels, which will give the impression of different whites. (The higher the gloss level, the lighter it looks.) Use a low-sheen acrylic for the walls, high-gloss enamel on the skirtings (and other trims) and a flat finish on the ceilings (you can use half strength on the ceiling if you want to lighten it up).

The Psychology of Colour

In 1918 the *Ladies Home Journal* reported 'the generally accepted rule is pink for the boy and blue for the girl'. It just goes to show how our perception of colour, to some extent, is driven by fashion. However, we also have genuine physiological responses to colour—so when choosing colour for the home, it's a good idea to consider not only how a colour looks, but also how it feels.

Black

Black is sophisticated and elegant, especially when contrasted with white. It works best when used sparingly as it will feel oppressive when overdone. If you'd like to use black on bigger surfaces such as walls, try a deep taupe or charcoal instead. As with brown, black looks fabulous on floors teamed with white walls.

Brown

Brown is earthy, natural and tranquil. One of the most popular interior choices is to team white walls with timber floors. The dark earthiness of the brown floorboards grounds the sense of spaciousness evoked by the whiteness of the walls, creating a perfect balance.

However, avoid using too much brown as it has a tendency to feel dull when not teamed with a lighter colour.

Green and blue

Green and blue are cool and calm and provoke a sense of peacefulness (just think of the greens and blues in nature). The paler shades are the most calming and certainly worth trying in the bedroom if you have a child who finds it hard to get to sleep.

(The only thing to be careful of is using a dull blue in a dark room, as it may feel depressive rather than serene—light shades in sunny rooms work the best.)

Greens and blues also work well in bathrooms and meditation rooms.

Orange and yellow

Orange and yellow are warm, happy colours and therefore work well in the more social areas of the home. Some brighter shades can be too stimulating in bedrooms, but perfect for kitchens, playrooms and family rooms.

Pink

Pink is the tint of red. Because it contains so much white it is much more gentle than red. It is a sweet, soft colour and in its paler forms is very relaxing. I think pink is perfect for little girls' bedrooms.

Red

Red is stimulating and exciting—studies show that looking at red increases our heart rate—therefore it's probably not a good idea to overdo it in a bedroom as it won't encourage sleep. However, used in small amounts, it's an amazing accent colour.

Violet and Purple

Violet and purple are unusual and extravagant colours. They are the colours favoured by royalty, religion and the suffragettes. Elegant and eye-catching, violets and purples are best suited to formal areas. They need to be used sparingly, or they may become overwhelming.

White

White gives a wonderful sense of spaciousness. White reflects light and sends it bouncing around a room, making it look bigger than it is. White symbolises innocence, cleanliness and purity—and is cooling in hot climates.

However, too much stark white will feel cold and clinical, so use warmer shades and team with natural materials and textiles.

Milk Paint

Milk paint is 100 per cent natural, non-toxic and biodegradable. It is one of the safest paints available (which makes it perfect for nurseries and children's rooms)—and with no 'paint' smell, it is a joy to use.

It is also possibly the world's oldest paint. Cave drawings and paintings, at least 8000 years old, have been found coloured in a simple form of milk paint made from milk, lime and earth pigment. For thousands of years, the recipe for milk paint remained relatively unchanged and the ingredients were readily available.

However, in the 1860s the invention of the metal paint can saw the beginning of the commercial paint industry. As milk paint, like all milk products, spoils fairly rapidly and must be made as needed rather than pre-mixed, it was oil-based paint (made with highly poisonous additives) that was mass-produced for the new industry.

Though many of the more dangerous chemicals have since been banned from synthetic paint, and paint companies are developing an increasing number of paints with lower VOCs (volatile organic compounds), it is still predominantly the natural paints, such as milk paint, which have no VOCs.

Milk paint can be made from scratch using casein powder (milk protein), pigment powder and water. However, for convenience it is easier to buy it commercially.

Either way, the paint is quite gorgeous to work with. You simply whisk the powder with water until it forms a creamy batter and leave to stand until it thickens a little. It will continue to thicken as you paint but, once dry, the finish is consistent and very smooth and can be sealed with natural beeswax.

Milk paint is velvety soft, both in colour and texture—and the end result is reminiscent of the traditional lime-washed walls seen in the likes of France and Italy.

Exterior Colours

When selecting exterior colours, avoid bright hues, as they have the tendency to look kitsch. The classic colours work best; try charcoals, taupes, biscuits, creams and off-whites. Avoid pure white, which looks too harsh. Two or three colours are more than enough; any more will look too busy.

Order for Painting an Entire Room

1. Cornices and ceilings—first coat

2. Walls—first coat

3. Cornices and ceilings—final coat

4. Skirtings, architraves and doors—first coat

5. Walls—final coat

6. Skirtings, architraves and doors—final coat

MIX AND USE MILK PAINT

Commercial milk paint comes as a powder that you mix up with water as you go. How much paint you mix up at a time comes down to a little guesswork, but I usually start with around three cups of powder. (If you have any mixture left over, you can cover it in plastic wrap and keep it in the fridge for up to 24 hours.)

WHAT YOU NEED

A bag of milk paint

2 bowls

A wooden spoon or whisk

A stocking or piece of muslin to strain
   with

A good-quality brush

Beeswax or clear sealer to seal

METHOD

1. Pour the powder into a bowl and mix with enough water to form a 'pancake batter' consistency. Whisk well to get all the lumps out.

2. Leave to thicken for 10 minutes.

3. Strain the mixture through a stocking into a second bowl (though as I didn't have any stockings, I used one of my daughter's old ballet tights, or you could use a piece of muslin).

4. You're now ready to paint. The mixture will continue to thicken as you work—and at times it will feel as if you are painting with yoghurt rather than milk—but once dry, the finish is consistent and very smooth.

5. Once the first coat is dry, sand lightly before applying the second coat.

6. Seal with natural beeswax or an all-purpose clear sealer.

Tips for painting walls

- Buy special removable masking tape from a paint shop—it's very depressing if you leave regular masking tape on too long and it leaves a mess when you try to take it off.
- Buy good-quality brushes. Cheaper brushes tend to lose more bristles—not a good look on your walls.
- Dip no more than a third of the brush into the paint at a time, gently wipe or tap excess paint back into the tin.
- 'Cutting in' with the brush before using the roller, gives the roller a little edge to work within, which prevents you accidentally painting the skirtings, etc.
- When using the roller, keep the edges wet to avoid overlap marks.

PAINT INTERIOR WALLS

If previously painted walls are in good condition—and aren't too high—they're very simple to re-paint.

WHAT YOU NEED

Sugar soap

Cloth

Drop sheets

Masking tape

Undercoat (optional)

Low-sheen acrylic paint

Paint brush

Roller and roller tray

METHOD

1. Clean walls thoroughly with sugar soap and a cloth and allow them to dry.

2. Drag furniture into the middle of the room and cover with drop sheets, apply masking tape to light fittings, power outlets and along skirtings and trims, and place more drop sheets on the ground.

3. Apply one coat of undercoat to seal and prime walls (in much the same way as you might apply a primer to your face before applying foundation). This step must be taken if walls are raw or in poor condition—however, you can skip this step if the walls are already painted AND are in perfect condition.

4. Apply the first coat of paint. Use a paintbrush to cut in along the edges, cornices and skirtings—use the roller to fill in the main part of the wall.

5. Allow the first coat to dry before applying the second coat.

French washed walls

A Note on Paint Types

Traditionally there were two basic paint types: acrylic (or water-based) paints and enamel (or oil-based) paints. However, due to the high toxicity of enamel paint, new water-based enamels have entered the market. Though some argue they're not quite as glossy and hardwearing as traditional oil-based enamels, water-based enamels are much less toxic and, therefore, a much better choice.

A Note on Cleaning Up

If you've been painting with water-based paints, you can rinse brushes, rollers and trays in the sink; if you've used oil-based paints, you will have to rinse off in turps.

If you have leftover paint, it must be thrown into the bin, rather than down the drain. However, as most councils won't allow you to throw liquid paint into your bin, you'll have to solidify it first. The easiest way to do this is by mixing in some kitty litter or sand.

FRENCH WASH WALLS

French washing is a very old, traditional technique, which adds subtle movement and a soft beauty to walls. This is a two-person project, both simple and fun.

For the best results, start in one spot and keep moving in one direction around the whole room until you're back at the beginning. You need to work fairly fast as the wash is quite runny.

WHAT YOU NEED

Sugar soap

Cloth

Low-sheen acrylic (base coat)

French wash

A large muslin cloth

Brush

METHOD

1. Clean and prepare wall thoroughly with sugar soap and a cloth and allow them to dry.

2. Apply two coats of the low-sheen acrylic and allow to dry.

3. Apply the French wash. This needs two people. The first person applies the French wash with a brush, using messy, multi-directional strokes (rather than nice up-and-down strokes). The second person follows with a muslin cloth, scrunched into a messy bundle, using it to gently dab the walls.

2.

Muslin cloth

FABULOUS FABRICS & WONDERFUL WALLPAPERS

how to select, hang and sew

Fabulous Fabrics

I have an absolute love affair with fabrics, especially cottons, linens and silks. Natural fabrics simply feel more beautiful than synthetics and I find myself intuitively drawn to them. They also tend to grow even more gorgeous with age and don't pill like man-made fibres do. My utopian home would have thick linen-covered sofas, organic cotton sheets and oversized silk curtains pooling onto the floor.

As deliciously tactile as natural fabrics are, I have to admit there are a few things to keep in mind if you choose to live with them. Natural fabrics have a tendency to crease, fade and stain. Not that that's necessarily a bad thing; a crushed linen curtain or a faded vintage silk cushion has a certain sensual appeal.

I remember bringing home a beautiful new blanket for my daughter when she was very little, and the first thing she did was spill strawberry on it. I started to worry about getting the stain out, when her grandmother stopped me by saying the red stain will just become part of the blanket's history. I love that; it's just such a relaxed philosophy to live with. And I still have that blanket.

However, as much as I admire the naturals, there is a place for synthetics. I almost always use a hardy synthetic on upholstery that can't be easily washed, such as a sofa. A full synthetic fabric is inherently stain-resistant and therefore particularly sensible for those with children or pets. The trick is to pick the right synthetic; I always select fabrics which have a thick linen-look weave, never anything that looks too shiny and, well, synthetic.

Natural fabrics also have a tendency to break down in the sun, so use acrylics on outdoor furniture (I love the bright French striped viscose canvas range by Toiles du Soleil) and always line natural curtains if they receive a lot of sun.

Viewing fabric in Mokum's Brisbane showroom.

Which Window Treatment?

Windows can be covered with curtains, blinds or shutters. In general, contemporary homes suit the clean lines of roller blinds; older homes, the classic look of roman blinds—and both can benefit from the softness of curtains.

Thick, full curtains should always be used in the bedroom, blinds and shutters always let in slithers of morning light. Extend your tracks at least 20 centimetres past the architraves and right down to the floor to make your curtains appear larger and lusher, and block every bit of light. Quite commonly, clients have a second smaller window above the bed; do not do a curtain in this case, a roman blind in the same fabric works better.

Roman blinds are stunning and can be very classic or extremely relaxed, depending on the fabric you use. If you're after a clean, timeless style, select a lined, linen fabric in a neutral shade. For a more relaxed look, unlined cotton works beautifully. (Though as mentioned, natural fabrics can eventually disintegrate in the sun—so only use unlined cotton on fairly shady windows. Alternatively, use inexpensive cotton that you don't mind replacing later.).

I find roller blinds the least interesting of all, but they work well in contemporary spaces where you don't want the window treatment to be prominent. For example, a recent client built on the beach and we wanted the water to stay the focal point of the design, so white rollers, which 'disappeared' into white walls, really worked. However, as rollers can feel quite sterile, we chose a large natural linen curtain for the main sliding door, to create a much cosier space.

A Note on Pre-Shrinking Fabric

It's a superb idea to make cushion covers, slipcovers, curtains and throws out of washable fabrics such as cotton and linen—however, as these fabrics will shrink by about three per cent after their first wash—you really need to wash them before you start sewing.

Simply soak the fabric in a tub of hot water for an hour or so—and then gently squeeze out the excess water before hanging out to dry (be careful to hang larger, heavier pieces over a couple of lines to prevent it from becoming misshapen).

Iron on the wrong side whilst still slightly damp.

After shot of raw linen envelope cushion.

After shot of raw linen envelope cushion with vintage
doily detail

ENVELOPE CUSHION, HAND SEWN

My sewing lady, Jane Wilson, came up with these superbly simple cushions, which require only two seams and take only minutes to make. As the use of hemming tape keeps the sewing to a minimum, this method is ideal for those who don't have a sewing machine. The beauty of an envelope cushion is that they don't require a zip—for beginners, like me, that's a bit of a blessing. The opening at the back of the cushion overlaps and you simply tuck the insert in.

Once the cushion is made, it can be embellished with decorative wooden buttons, French-style braiding or a vintage doily if desired.

WHAT YOU NEED

Half a metre of fabric (we've used raw linen)

Needle and thread

Hemming tape

Pencil

Tape measure, scissors and pins

METHOD

1. Mark and then cut your fabric so that it measures 47 x 110cm (18.8 x 44in) wide.

2. Neaten the side edges (47cm/18.8in edges) with a 1cm-wide (0.4in) hemming tape. (Simply fold a 1–2cm/0.4–0.8in flap over the tape and iron).

3. Lay the linen right side up and fold the sides in evenly until the cushion measures 45cms (18in) wide.

4. Pin across the top and bottom (1cm/0.4in) and sew.

5. Overlock and then turn right side out.

ENVELOPE CUSHION, MACHINE SEWN

The measurements given are for 45 x 45 centimetre (18 inch) cushions (a fairly regular-sized throw cushion) and they allow for a 15 centimetre (6 inch) overlap—however, you can adjust as desired to make different-sized cushions.

WHAT YOU NEED

Half a metre of fabric

Thread

Tape measure, scissors and pins

METHOD

1. Cut out a piece of fabric 47 x 47cm (19in) for the front of the cushion and two pieces, 39.5 x 47cm (16 x 19in) and 24.5 x 47cm (10 x 19in) for the back (one piece is bigger to allow for the opening to overlap).

2. Along one 47cm (19in) edge of each back piece; iron and sew a 1cm (0.4in) seam.

3. Lay the back pieces on top of the front piece—right sides together with the back seams overlapping in the middle.

4. Pin and sew all the way around the edge of the cushion. Turn out.

Plain

Piped

Flanged

ENVELOPE CUSHION, WITH A FLANGE

This is a gorgeous variation of the basic machine-sewn envelope cushion we've made on the previous page. You simply add an extra 6 centimetres (2.5in) of material the entire way around the cushion to create the flange.

WHAT YOU NEED

60 centimetres (24in) of fabric

Thread

Tape measure, scissors and pins

METHOD

1. Cut out a piece of fabric 59 x 59cm (23.6in) for the front of the cushion. And two pieces, 45.5 x 59cm (18.2 x 23.6in) and 30.5 x 59cm (12.2 x 23.6in) for the back.

2. Along one 59cm (23.6in) edge of each back piece iron and sew a 1cm (0.4in) seam.

3. Lay the back pieces on top of the front piece—right sides together with the back seams overlapping in the middle.

4. Pin and sew around the edge of the cushion. Turn right side out.

5. On the right side—pin and sew a second seam, 6cm (2.5in) in from the edge, to create the flange.

ENVELOPE CUSHION, WITH PIPING

In this variation, the process and measurements are very similar to the machine-sewn envelope cushion, except you attach piping to the front panel of the cushion before you sew the front and backs together.

WHAT YOU NEED

Half a metre of fabric

2 metres (6.56 feet) of piping

Thread

Tape measure, scissors and pins

METHOD

1. Cut out a piece of fabric 47 x 47cm (18.8in) for the front of the cushion. And two pieces, 39.5 x 47cm (15.8 x 18.8in) and 24.5 x 47cm (9.8 x 18.8in) for the back.

2. Along one 47cm (18.8in) edge of each back piece; iron and sew a 1cm (0.4in) seam.

3. Pin the piping onto the front piece of fabric. You will have to carefully snip the piping four or five times to allow it to turn around the corners. Use the piping foot on your machine to sew the piping on.

4. Lay the front fabric on top of the back pieces, right sides together, and pin carefully. Use your piping foot again to sew the front and back pieces together. Sew from the front so you can follow the line of stitching. Turn out.

SIMPLE SHEER CURTAIN

A simple sheer curtain helps to diffuse bright sunlight without completely blocking breezes or a view.

WHAT YOU NEED

Sheer fabric

Spring clips with rings (available from
    sewing shops)

Thread

Tape measure, scissors and pins

METHOD

1. Measure your window from the rod to the floor. This is your drop; add 22cm (8.8in) for hemming and seams. The width of your fabric needs to be wider than your window (twice as wide is good if you can manage it).

2. Pin and sew a 1cm (0.4in) seam around the entire piece of fabric.

3. Turn over the top by 10cm (4in) and hem.

4. Turn over the bottom by 10cm (4in) and hem.

5. Attach to rod with the spring clips.

UNLINED LINEN CURTAIN

If I need very elegant fully-lined curtains, I always have them professionally made—generally with a pencil-pleat heading and hung on a rod with gliders, so that they open and close beautifully.

However, for a more relaxed style, these unlined linen curtains are perfect—and so easy to make

WHAT YOU NEED

Linen

Thread

Tape measure, scissors and pins

METHOD

1. Pin and sew a 1cm (0.4in) seam around all edges

2. Turn over the top by 10cm (4in) and hem.

3. Pin and sew a 5cm (2in) seam running parallel to the hem. (Check your rod is narrow enough to fit through a 5cm/2in hem, or adjust the seam size accordingly).

4. Turn over the bottom by 10cm (4in) and hem.

1.

2.

3.

4.

5cm

SILK THROW

WHAT YOU NEED

4 metres (13.1 feet) of silk (approximately
140 centimetres (55.1 inches) wide)
2 metres (6.56 feet) of wadding (cut to
the same width as the silk)
Silk thread
Scissors, pins, needle
Sewing machine

METHOD

1. Cut two pieces of silk, 2m (6.56f) x width of fabric.

2. Layer the two pieces of silk on top of one another—and then layer the piece of wadding on top.

3. Pin and sew around three edges—leaving one narrow edge open.

4. Turn right side out (as you would with a doona cover). The wadding layer should now be sandwiched between the two pieces of silk.

5. Turn under the raw edges of the open end—and machine stitch across the top to close.

6. Measure and pin 10cm (4in) rows across the width of the throw. Hand-sew the layers together using a simple running stitch.

A Note on Wadding

Wadding is the soft layer of padding sewn into quilts to keep them warm and comfy. We used bamboo wadding for this project, but you can also find cotton, wool or polyester wadding. It's sold either buy the metre or in pieces, and it's available from fabric and quilting stores.

Another green alternative to bamboo is corn wadding.

The finished silk throw.

UPHOLSTERED LINEN BEDHEAD

This is surprisingly easy and quite enjoyable to make. The trick is to use a very lightweight upholstery fabric, perhaps a linen or linen/cotton blend, as anything heavier is too hard to get neat at the corners.

Also, it's easiest to work on a nice big table if you can.

MOUNTING THE HEADBOARD

Mount your headboard onto the wall using keyhole brackets and screws (available from your local hardware store). You'll need to fix them into your wall studs—if you can't find the wall studs, you'll need to buy hollow wall anchors as well.

WHAT YOU NEED

MDF board, 1600 x 900 centimetres (640 x 360 inches) (Ask your local hardware store if they can cut to size.)

50 millimetre thick foam, 1600 x 900 centimetres (640 x 360 inches) (Your local foam store may be able to cut foam to size on the spot.)

Wadding, 2 metres (80 inches) (available from fabric stores)

Fabric, 2 metres (80 inches)

Double-sided tape

Staple gun

METHOD

1. Attach the foam to the MDF board with double-sided tape.

2. Lay the board, foam side down, on to the wadding. Wrap the wadding firmly around the board and staple to the back. It's easiest to start with a staple to the middle of each edge and each corner, and then go back around adding more staples. If the wadding is too bulky in the corners, trim with scissors. Trim any other excess wadding.

3. Repeat this process with the fabric.

BUTTONED BEDHEAD

A deep diamond-buttoned bedhead is the ultimate in luxury. It's not really a home project as it takes years to perfect the skill required for true diamond-buttoning.

However, with the kind help of Denise Kennedy, a soft furnishings expert and owner of Curtain Elegance, we've come up with a simple version, which mimics the real thing.

WHAT YOU NEED

Drill

Buttoning kit (12 buttons)

Left-over fabric from your bedhead

Darning needle, cord

METHOD

1. Make your bedhead as per the instructions on the previous page, except drill twelve evenly spaced holes into the MDF board before you start.

2. Cover your buttons as per the instructions on the pack.

3. Attach the buttons with the darning needle and cord. Start at the back of each pre-cut hole and push the threaded darning needle through to sew on the button, tie off and then staple at the back.

1.

3a.

3b.

3c.

3d.

3e.

After

A Note on MDF

As previously mentioned, MDF isn't the healthiest option for furniture—however, you can seal MDF with a coat of natural paint to prevent it from 'off-gassing', or source E0 particleboard and use in lieu of MDF.

Wonderful Wallpaper

I love that the golden years of wallpaper were in the roaring 20s—for no other reason than it's an era I adore—and I am thrilled wallpaper is back in fashion. Papering a room adds instant opulence. Three rolls of Osborne and Little and a plain little powder room becomes something else entirely.

The master bedroom is my most favourite place to paper, there's something just so deliciously decadent about it. Paper the entire room rather than picking out a feature wall, the result will be much more striking. A patterned paper looks particularly divine when highlighted by fresh white skirtings and trims.

Wallpapers are no longer made only from paper; they are now also made from vinyl, bamboo, cotton, foil and numerous other materials. Though I still consider papers the prettiest, vinyls are excellent for areas that receive more wear and tear as they are hardier and washable, whilst grass-weaves work perfectly in natural-style interiors.

Hanging wallpaper well is an art form, and with a roll of designer papers costing quite a lot, I almost always recommend using a professional (the only exception being if it's a very small and simple wall—and you use one of the newer non-woven wallpapers which require you to paste the wall not the paper—much easier! See How-to hang non-woven wallpaper on page 126 for details).

Once you find a piece of fabric or wallpaper you absolutely love, be daring enough to decorate around it. It'll bring you joy every day.

Colour and Pattern

Once you find a piece of fabric or wallpaper you absolutely love, be daring enough to decorate around it. Select one of the neutral colours in the design to use as the restful colour in the room. Use this neutral colour on painted walls or perhaps the carpet. Select the most brilliant colour in the pattern to use as your accent colour. Use this colour in art, accessories and soft furnishings.

Eyes need places to rest, so it is important to have clear spaces between patterned objects. Therefore, as a general rule, look at the main elements of the room and balance the patterned with the plain. For example, if the walls are patterned keep the floors plain.

To successfully group different patterns together, simply establish a theme based on colour, texture or design. This works particularly well when different but complimentary fabrics are used in close proximity to one another, as happens commonly with cushions.

HANG NON-WOVEN WALLPAPER

Wallpapers made from paper, vinyl and grasses are quite tricky to hang—newer non-woven papers are much easier, as you paste the wall rather than the paper.

Start with a simple, straightforward wall with no obstacles (perhaps a feature wall in a bedroom—do not start with a bathroom as going around a toilet is tricky!).

Wallpaper is generally sold in rolls that are 53 centimetres (21 inches) wide and 10 metres (33 feet) long. An average wall will need two to three rolls of paper (a good tip is to check the batch numbers on the rolls, as the colours can differ quite substantially between batches).

The other great thing about non-woven wallpapers is they're dry-strippable—which makes them very easy to remove or replace when the time comes.

WHAT YOU NEED

Wallboard sealer

Sandpaper

Wallpaper size (available from wallpaper stores, its purpose is help prepare the walls)

Wallpaper

Wallpaper paste

Scissors

Roller

Straight edge spreader (a plastic tool to help smooth the paper)

Rag

Sharp knife (or Stanley knife)

Ruler (preferably with a handle to make cutting easier)

METHOD

1. Prepare the surface. If it's a new build with bare gyprock walls, seal the surface with a wallboard sealer. If the walls are painted with an acrylic paint, simply sand lightly.

2. Apply a coat of size to the wall. (Size is available from wallpaper stores and some hardware stores. Its purpose is to even up the porosity of the wall—it also gives a little bit of slip, allowing you to more easily slide the wallpaper sideways to line up patterns.)

3. Cut the wallpaper to length, allowing for overlap on both the top and bottom.

4. Apply the paste to the wall with a roller, cut in with a brush where required (if you accidently get some glue on the cornice or ceiling, don't worry, just wipe it off with a rag after you've trimmed the paper).

5. Hang the wallpaper from the top to the bottom of the wall—smoothing the paper over with a straight edge spreader as you go.

6. Trim paper along the top and bottom with a thin, sharp knife and a ruler (a ruler with a handle is easier—the ruler needs to be longer than the width of the wallpaper).

7. Repeat until the wall is done.

Vintage Note

Before commercial wallpaper glues were readily available, wallpaper hangers used to make their own glue with flour and water. This used to work perfectly well in England, but when they tried it in Australia, cockroaches kept eating through the paper to get to the flour!

FOUND
FURNITURE
how to source, restore and adore

A vintage deep-buttoned tub chair is given a new lease of life thanks to the expert craftsmanship of Steven Williams, whose family has owned and operated Parry & Williams Upholsterers since 1959

Finding and Fixing

Avoid mundane mass-produced MDF furniture and source quality old pieces instead, which you can revamp with fresh fabric, stain and paint. You'll not only end up with more interesting and eclectic pieces, but also pieces with more soul.

The best places to source affordable vintage furniture are garage sales, charity shops and by the roadside. Don't look at the tatty old fabric or a bad paint job; look at the shape and structure. You must love the shape from the beginning, as that won't change. The structure must be sound, or it could prove too difficult and costly to fix.

Don't rush in and paint a piece until you find out what it is first. If it's a genuine antique, you could severely depreciate its value if you don't restore it correctly.

If you have an everyday piece, be as daring as you like with your choices—you can't ruin it (and even if everything goes horribly wrong, you can always start again).

Restoring Antique Pieces

Andrew Baxter, from Baxter's Antique Restorations, has been restoring antiques for over 30 years. He advises that each piece must be individually assessed to determine the correct method of restoration required—but generally, restoration falls into one of the following four categories:

Revive and Wax

This method is for pieces that are in good condition, but just need a clean and polish. It achieves the same result as stripping and polishing, but is much faster and easier to do. (The vintage frame on page 140 took us one hour; it would have taken a day to strip and stain.) Use a good-quality commercially used reviver and wax.

Spot Strip

If only part of the piece is damaged, such as the top of a desk, Andrew will restore that section fully and then revive and wax the remainder. This is obviously less costly and quicker than restoring the entire piece.

Shellac and Wax

A shellac and wax is the quick version of a full restoration. It won't quite achieve the same full depth and body in the finish, but it will nicely freshen up the polish. Wash the old shellac or varnish off with stripper and then methylated spirits. Lightly sand before applying two new coats of shellac. Protect the finish with two coats of wax.

Full Restoration

For pieces that have been badly neglected and/or exposed to the elements a full restoration may be required. Strip, sand and prepare the piece for finishing by repairing any minor damage, filling any small holes and finishing with a product of your choice.

VINTAGE FRAME (REVIVE AND WAX)

This beautiful 1920s frame features exquisite hand-stamped details—it was picked up at a charity shop. As it was structurally sound, it only needed to be revived and waxed.

WHAT YOU NEED

Small craft knife

Reviver (we used a furniture reviver)

Fine-grade (0000) steel wool

Soft cloths

Toothbrush

Wax (we used Furniture Wax)

Gloves

METHOD

1. Use a small craft or Stanley knife to gently scrape off any lumps of dirt (or more likely, spider poo!). Be very careful not to cut through the finish.

2. Apply the reviver with the fine-grade steel wool. It's important to follow the grain so you don't scratch the timber—and keep your strokes long and even. Use the reviver sparingly, and wipe off any excess as you go with a soft cloth.

3. Go over with a toothbrush, working in a circular motion to get into any intricately carved or moulded areas. Wipe off excess reviver.

4. Apply the wax sparingly with the steel wool (the more you put on the more you'll have to take off). Wear gloves to protect your hands and to prevent your nails being stained with black.

5. Leave to dry for approximately 10 minutes.

6. Burnish off with a soft clean rag (an old t-shirt is perfect).

before

1.

3.

4.

5.

6.

After

A Note on Burnishing

Burnishing just means to polish—the idea is to rub quite fast so that the wax heats up and softens as you work. This process can be repeated up to half a dozen times or until you're happy with the result. Allow the wax to dry for around an hour between coats.

before

2.

3.

4.

CARD FILE DRAWERS (REVIVE AND WAX)

I found this English oak card file drawer at my local charity shop. It had originally been used to file cards at a public library.

Card file drawers usually have slat bottoms, so small objects fall through. To rectify this, simply cut out a piece of plywood and lay it inside the drawer (I just used a piece of thick cardboard and some scissors—even easier!).

Though the finish wasn't perfect I liked its slightly worn appearance, so, like the frame, it only received a quick revive and wax. However, I did want to change the plastic knobs for metal handles (big enough to cover the original nameplate marks).

WHAT YOU NEED

Ruler

Bradawl

Drill and drill bits

Screwdriver

New handles to replace the original

METHOD

1. Remove the old knobs.

2. Use a ruler to check the new handles are centred, and mark with a bradawl (a small tool used to punch through, or in this case mark, timber, leather and other materials).

3. Use a hand or cordless drill to drill the required holes.

4. Screw on your handles (if the screws are a little hard to get in, coat them with a little soap or candle wax).

EUROPEAN BEDSIDE

Found at a local garage sale, this bedside cabinet was originally from Europe and made from a fruit tree. The plug style knob and rustic finish made it look decidedly 'country'—but it just needed a dark stain and new crystal-style knob to dress it up.

Look for enviromentally friendly, plant-based, non-toxic, polyurethane-free wood stains.

WHAT YOU NEED

Fine hand saw

Screwdriver

Chemical stripper, gloves and safety
    glasses

Methylated spirits

steel wool (00 and 0000 grade)

Sandpaper (150- 240- and 400-grit)

Dark wood stain (we used walnut)

Shellac

Paintbrush

Furniture wax

Bradawl, drill and drill bits

New crystal-style knob

METHOD

1. Use a hand saw to remove the wooden knob.

2. Use a screwdriver to remove fixtures from cabinet (hinges and catch) so that the cabinet door comes away.

3. Chemically strip the bedside cabinet carefully, following the manufacturer's instructions. Safety is paramount when using chemical strippers—wear industrial-strength rubber gloves, safety glasses and work in a well-ventilated area.

4. Neutralise paint stripper by washing off with methylated spirits and 00 steel wool, ensuring that you wipe off residue (methylated spirits will also evaporate fast and dry the timber, so you'll be able to work on your piece again straight away).

5. Lightly sand timber surfaces, first with 150-grit sandpaper, then with a finer 240-grit sandpaper to end with a smooth finish. (Always sand with the grain—if you sand against the grain scratches will show through after the finish is applied.)

after

6. Apply stain evenly with a clean rag and allow to dry.

7. Apply a fine coat of shellac with a paintbrush, enabling it to dry and recoat if necessary, cutting back between coats with 400-grade sandpaper.

8. Cut back shellac finish with 0000 grade steel wool so it has an even dull appearance, and then finish it off with the wax.

9. Use a pencil to mark where the new crystal-style knob is to go. Spike the surface with a bradawl, this ensures the drill bit will not drift when starting to drill your hole. Drill your hole and then screw your new knob into position

10. Reattach the door to the bedside.

ANTIQUE 1920S CARVER (FULL RESTORATION)

This gorgeous old boy was found under a house and it was absolutely covered in 20 years' worth of dust. Under all the dirt and grime though, was a beautiful solid maple chair with a walnut-veneered back.

Unfortunately, as it had been exposed to the weather, the finish was damaged and the chair needed to be fully restored. Andrew and one of his tradesmen, Michael, were kind enough to take on this job (it's not for the faint-hearted).

WHAT YOU NEED

Furniture Reviver

Chemical stripper, rubber gloves and
    safety glasses

Methylated spirits

Sandpaper (150-, 240- and 400-grit)

Wood stop (putty) in colour to match stain

Wood stain in colour of your choice

Soft cloths

00 and 0000 grade steel wool

Shellac

Paintbrush

Furniture wax

METHOD

1. Try and revive—hopefully that will leave you with a smooth and clean finish. If that method doesn't work and the surface is still rough or too crazed—stripping and washing off with meths will be required.

2. Chemically strip the piece, carefully following the manufacturer's instructions. Safety is paramount when using chemical strippers—wear industrial-strength rubber gloves and safety glasses and work in a well-ventilated area.

3. Neutralise paint stripper by wiping over with methylated spirits soaked in a soft cloth (spirits will also evaporate fast and dry the timber, so you'll be able to work on your piece again straight away).

4. Lightly sand timber surfaces, first with 150-grit sandpaper, then with a finer 240-grit sandpaper to end with a smooth finish. (Always sand with the grain—if you sand against the grain scratches will show through after the finish is applied.)

9.

5. Fill in any holes with wood stop (in the same colour as the finish). When the filler is dry, lightly sand back with 240-grit sandpaper. Dust off all surfaces.

6. Apply stain evenly to the chair and allow to dry.

7. Apply three coats of shellac by brush, lightly sanding with 400-grit sandpaper between each coat.

8. Prepare for waxing by lightly sanding the topcoat with 400-grit sandpaper and then 00-grade steel wool. This will ensure a smooth, clean surface.

9. Apply wax with 0000-grade steel wool; allow to dry for 15–20 minutes, before burnishing off with a clean, soft cloth.

RE-COVER A DROP SEAT

Drop seats just pop in and out of the chair—and therefore are very easy to re-cover. If the foam and webbing are in good condition, you just need to tear off the old fabric and staple on the new.

However, in this case we needed to replace the foam and webbing as well.

WHAT YOU NEED

Staple gun

Webbing

Foam, cut to size

Glue

Fabric

METHOD

1. Remove old fabric, stuffing and webbing, leaving just the frame intact.

2. Use a staple gun to attach the new webbing. Start by attaching rows running in one direction, and then weave more rows through running in the other direction.

3. Glue the foam onto the frame.

4. Place the frame face-down onto the fabric. Wrap and staple.

2a.

2b.

3.

4.

after

Revamping Everyday Pieces

This is where you get to be more daring in your design choices. Transforming a piece from frumpy to fabulous is enormous fun—and it's even more satisfying when it costs next to nothing.

Sanding versus Stripping

Good painting is all in the preparation. Unfortunately, the preparation is tedious, but it must be done, and done well. You can remove old paint by sanding or by chemically stripping. Sanding is generally the easiest option for smaller jobs—however, strippers may be more effective for fiddly areas or when there's a thick build-up of paint.

If you are going to sand a vintage piece of furniture, keep in mind that most paints used until 1970 contained lead, so if you think there's any chance of there being lead paint on the furniture, check before sanding. You can do this by buying a very cheap and simple-to-use lead testing kit at your local paint shop.

I'm cautious of using traditional chemical strippers at home because of their high toxicity; however, there are now some great natural citrus-based strippers on the market, which are much safer to work with. The trick is to neutralise the paint stripper with methylated spirits after you've used it, otherwise the fresh paint won't adhere properly (she says from bitter experience!).

before

A Note on Painting Antiques

As beautiful as old timber is, sometimes the dark colours can be too heavy for certain rooms. If you want to paint an antique piece without devaluing it, the trick is to leave the old finish on to protect the wood—and use an oil-based enamel.

The reason for using an oil-based enamel is that it is easy to chemically strip, should you ever want to restore the piece later—whereas water-based paints need to be sanded, which can be detrimental to delicate moldings.

The bad news is oil-based enamels are pretty toxic; however, if you think it's worth preserving the original finish on an antique piece, here's how to do it.

Clean the piece with turpentine and steel wool. Wipe over with a damp cloth to remove any excess and allow to dry. Gently sand with a fine sandpaper—be careful to go with the grain so you don't scratch the finish. Apply two coats of enamel paint.

VINTAGE KITCHEN CHAIRS (HIGH-GLOSS FINISH)

This common vintage kitchen chair was bought at a garage sale for only a few dollars. I know some people would love its 'Shabby Chic' appeal, but it was too rough for me—I love finishes to be smooth and tactile. It was also far too dirty and needed a good clean.

WHAT YOU NEED

Sugar soap and a cloth
Sandpaper
High-gloss water-based enamel

METHOD

1. Clean thoroughly with sugar soap and warm water and allow it to dry.

2. Sand back until smooth and then wipe away any dust.

3. Apply two coats of high-gloss water-based enamel (the higher the gloss, the hardier the paint, which is good for a kitchen chair).

after

before

2a.

2b.

after

Chocolate
mud cup
cakes &
Strawberries
Yum!

RAW PINE STOOL (BLACK WOOD WASH)

This little solid pine stool was picked up cheaply from IKEA. The beauty of buying raw pine pieces is that they're so easy to up-cycle. Just ensure that the timber is raw and doesn't have a clear seal on it—and you're good to go.

WHAT YOU NEED

Sandpaper

Black wood wash, paintbrush

Soft cloth

Clear sealer (if a hardier finish is desired)

METHOD

1. Very lightly sand the stool, just enough to allow the wash to stick.

2. Apply the wash with a paintbrush, wiping off any excess with a soft cloth as you go. Repeat this process if a deeper colour is desired.

Tip This will leave a natural matt finish—if you prefer a glossier, hardier surface, seal with an all-purpose clear sealer.

INDUSTRIAL LOCKER (RUST FINISH)

Vintage industrial furniture adds masculinity and drama to an interior. You can find genuine aged and weather-beaten pieces, but they're generally quite pricey.

A more economical way to achieve this look is to buy a simple locker (ours was purchased from an office supply store) and use a liquid iron and instant rust to create an authentic rusted iron effect.

The result is utterly divine and the process is simple.

WHAT YOU NEED

Undercoat

Liquid iron

Instant rust

Clear Sealer

Brushes and rags

METHOD

1. Roughly sand the locker and apply one coat of undercoat

2. Apply two coats of liquid iron by brush—allow twelve hours drying time between coats (don't overly worry about how neat your painting is, it won't matter as long as the locker is covered).

3. Apply instant rust when the second coat of Liquid Iron is touch dry (you can play around until you reach the level of rust you're happy with—the more instant rust you apply, the more rust you'll get).

4. Allow two days to dry before applying a clear sealer.

1.

2.

3.

after

80S-STYLE DESK ('AGED' FINISH)

Anastasia's husband, Jason, restored this old 80s-style desk for her, using two shades of milk paint and beeswax. This technique produces a beautifully 'aged' finish.

The undercoat you get does need to be suitable for milk paint. In this project, Porter's milk paint in Provencale was used as the base colour and Sableux as the second colour.

WHAT YOU NEED

Screwdriver

Sandpaper

Undercoat

Good-quality paintbrushes

2 shades of milk paint, base colour and
    second colour

Beeswax and toothbrush

Spatula and brushes

Fine-grade steel wool

Clear water-based sealer and bamboo
    skewer

Black pigment

METHOD

1. Remove the handles with a screwdriver, sand thoroughly and wipe down.

2. Apply one coat of undercoat with a brush.

3. Apply two coats of your chosen base colour. Sand lightly between coats.

4. Use a toothbrush to apply a small amount of beeswax to the areas you'd like the base colour to show through. It's a good idea to choose areas that will naturally age faster, such as the corners, edges and around the handles.

5. Apply two coats of your second colour of milk paint.

6. Gently scrape waxed areas with a spatula, and then a fine-grade steel wool, to reveal the base colour.

7. To create an aged finish, pour clear sealer into a jar and use a bamboo skewer to add a small amount of black pigment. To mix, shake vigorously with the lid on.

8. Apply two coats of sealer.

9. Screw in new handles.

DAILY
DECADENCE
the little things in life

VINIERS of Sheffield
& ELECTRO PLATED NICKLED SILVER
1930's
COMPLETE SET
$ 100.00

Vintage Pleasures

It's so easy to live with old-world decadence in the home. Eat with real silver, sip from bone china and sleep in vintage linen—it often costs no more and gives great pleasure.

Real Silver

There are three main types of vintage silver you can collect: sterling silver, silverplate and EPNS. Sterling silver is almost 100 per cent silver, very soft and very expensive; silverplate is a thin layer of silver, which is applied to a base metal, it looks just as beautiful as sterling silver, but is much more affordable (Sheffield is the most highly sought silverplate); EPNS is electroplated nickel silver, a newer method (developed in the mid-1800s) of silver plating.

Though (or perhaps because) it's usually the least expensive, I actually like buying EPNS cutlery as it requires much less maintenance—in fact I throw my ESPN cutlery in the dishwasher—and so far no problems (however, I should mention antique dealers and serious collectors would definitely disapprove). Silver and silverplate, on the other hand, need to be hand-washed and polished regularly.

If you buy silver that is slightly gold or yellow, that's just light tarnish and it's easy to get off. Simply apply a non-abrasive cream polish, apply and rinse off as per instructions. Buy a good-quality polish from a silversmith or jewellers. Don't try the numerous homemade recipes for polishing silver, as many contain ingredients such as baking soda and toothpaste, which are too abrasive.

If the silver is really black, it is either severely tarnished, and it'll be harder to get off, or the silver plate may have worn down to the base metal. If this is the case, you can have the flatware professionally re-plated, but as this is quite an expensive process it may be better to source less worn pieces.

Vintage silver looks divinely decadent on a table, and I love how eating from my ornate silver cutlery makes every meal so much more special (and on the rare occasions I hand-wash itmo, I even enjoy the washing up more!).

Fine Bone China

Josiah Spode (of Spode china fame) added animal bone to their china recipe in the early 1800s and created one of the lightest and most translucent, but most durable china ever made. The delicate beauty of bone china makes it hard to believe it's actually quite strong, but it is—it breaks and chips far less easily than inferior china, which is probably why so much vintage china is still around.

It may be hideously expensive to buy a complete set (vintage or new) but it costs next to nothing to build your own 'crazy set' by collecting one-off pieces from garage sales and charity and second-hand stores. I actually prefer a mismatched setting; it's just so enjoyable looking at so many different beautiful pieces. To test the quality of bone china, lift it up to the light and place your hand behind it. If you can see your hand through the china, it is a good-quality piece.

Though you're supposed to wash fine china by hand, I've been washing mine in the dishwasher for years; I figure it's better to use and enjoy it without worrying about it too much, which is why buying precious but inexpensive pieces is so brilliant. A good trick is to use half dishwashing powder and half baking soda in the dishwasher. It's a bit gentler on the china (and better for the environment as well).

When tea was first imported to England, it was so prohibitively expensive, only the aristocracy could afford to drink it—and only the aristocracy could afford bone china; it's a gorgeous thought that for very little money we can sit down and enjoy quality loose-leaf tea served in an antique bone china teacup every day.

Elegant Glass and Cut Crystal

Vintage crystal and glassware looks gorgeous on a table. I especially love Elegant Glassware in cranberry and ruby shades. Elegant Glass was produced at the same time as Depression Glass; but is much finer and more expensive. Depression Glass was made cheaply by machine, and it's thick and heavy, whereas Elegant Glass was made, at least partially, by hand and it's light and delicate. It was originally sold in up-market department and jewellery stores, as opposed to Depression Glass, which was sold in 5- and 10-cent shops.

A few pieces of vintage cut crystal never go astray either. Source crystal from charity shops for the best prices. To test whether a piece is crystal, flick the rim gently but firmly with your finger—you should hear a beautiful musical ring.

Vintage Linen

Linen is one of the world's oldest luxury fabrics. All towels, tablecloths, napkins and bedding used to be made of linen (which is where the term comes from). Though the poor had to put up with rough, raw linen, the wealthy were able to afford the finest linen, which was usually beautifully embroidered and pure white.

Though it's not easy to find larger unmarked pieces such as tablecloths and sheeting—it's easy enough to find smaller pieces, which can then be stitched together to make a throw, or sewn onto new linen as a beautiful detail.

When caring for vintage linen, use gentle soaps and avoid chlorine-bleach as it will damage the fibres and make the fabric feel coarse. Hanging white linen in the sun helps to keep it white.

Modern Pleasures

The most decadent modern pleasure I can think of is a great, big comfortable bed! Buy the best mattress you can afford and invest in fine linen—you'll be rewarded over and over.

Mattresses

Historically, mattresses were made from straw or animal hair, which was a breeding ground for all sorts of vermin. Today's offerings are much more hygienic and comfortable and can be quite luxurious..

Selecting a mattress is very personal. It is important to try them out. Lie on your back and try to slide your hand under the small of your back. If you easily achieve this, the mattress is too firm. Lie on your side; your body should sink into the mattress just enough so your spine is still straight. Stay on the mattress for at least 10 minutes to make sure you are comfortable.

Innerspring

Innerspring mattresses have been around since 1925 and have remained fundamentally unchanged for over 80 years.

The wire springs are what predominantly supports your body, while the padding and filling provide the comfort. Though there are several types of spring shapes available, pocket-springs are considered the best. This is because each spring is encased in its own fabric pocket and works independently to the other springs—so weight on one spring does not affect the rest of the mattress. Other spring systems to consider are hourglass and continuous coil. A good queen-size bed should have at least 375 springs.

What fills the mattress greatly determines the comfort and price. At the luxurious end of the market mattresses may be filled with silk, wool and cashmere. At the lower end, filling may consist of lower grades of foam, reclaimed cotton fibres and coconut fibre.

Despite guarantees of up to 25 years, mattresses need to be replaced at least every 10 years for hygiene reasons. Therefore more expensive mattresses will not necessarily last you longer, but will provide more luxury and comfort.

Latex

The sap of the rubber tree is the primary ingredient in this natural mattress that is inherently dust-mite resistant, anti-bacterial and breathable. This makes it an excellent choice for people who suffer from asthma or allergies.

In keeping with the desire to create a truly natural bed, some latex bed manufacturers even offer the mattress covered in natural materials such as organic cotton and wool. However, take care not to buy 'latex mattresses' that contain only a small amount of latex and are filled with sand and clay—buy from a specialist natural bedding company or reputable bedding store—and buy 100 per cent latex.

Memory Foam

Viscoelastic, or memory foam, was invented by NASA over 30 years ago to keep astronauts comfortable in zero gravity. Unlike other foams, which always want to spring back to their original shape, memory foam forms and retains an exact mould of your shape.

This eliminates any pressure points and gives a sense of weightlessness. Many medical practitioners, including orthopaedic surgeons, have found the 'low gravity' concept of memory foam is extremely beneficial to patients with back, neck and shoulder pain—so worth trying if you fall into this group.

Luxury Linen

High-quality linen is one of the most pleasurable daily luxuries you could invest in—and though initially the cost may be heart-stopping—it's made to last and will pay for itself in time.

The high-end brands are always made from quality natural fibres, which feel the most decadent against the skin and won't pile like cheap synthetics. Egyptian cotton is perhaps the most common luxury fibre for sheeting, followed by linen and silk.

There are also some new natural fabrics entering the luxury linen market—in particular, bamboo, which has a lovely silky sheen, and soybean, which is so soft it's often referred to as 'vegetable cashmere'.

The thread count is important and should be at least 300—however, be wary of clever marketing that overemphasises thread count but places no importance on thread quality. A high thread count of a cheap synthetic does not make a luxury sheet.

One of my favourite linen houses is Frette, who don't even list the thread count, preferring to concentrate on fibre quality and workmanship instead. They have an amazing history and have supplied the likes of the Italian Royal Family, the Ritz, the Orient Express and the Titanic.

Alternatively, seek out genuine vintage linen sheeting. The fibres in linen become softer and more beautiful with washing and use, and so the ageing of the fabric only adds to its appeal. Antique stores occasionally sell good-quality old linen, but as it is hard to come by it may be easier to look online. Antiquelinen.com sells pieces from c1800 to c1920. Expect to pay $145 for a 1920s Italian linen pillowcase. The prices for good sets can soar into the thousands. (New 100 per cent linen sheets are also hard to find in stores—but, again, easier to find online.)

VINTAGE CHINA CHOCOLATE STAND

One of my favourite decadences of all is chocolate, always dark of course and preferably served with champagne. To make the experience really divine, create a chocolate stand using small china teacups…

WHAT YOU NEED

Three china teacups and saucers
Craft glue (non-toxic)

METHOD

1. There is really only one step as you simply glue the china in place. The important thing to remember is the handles on the cups must sit flush (many don't) or else they won't stack properly. If you like, you can glue only two of the cups and saucers together and balance the other on top—this makes the washing up a little easier.

VINTAGE LINEN DETAIL

Vintage handmade hankies and napkins can be sewn onto fresh white linen to create beautifully detailed and interesting pieces. I've found charity stores are the best places to source vintage pieces, and they don't cost much at all. This is a very relaxing and easy project to do.

WHAT YOU NEED

A selection of white vintage cotton and
    linen hankies and napkins
White pillowcase or sheet
White cotton and a needle

METHOD

1. Simply place the hankies onto the linen as you desire; pin into place, and hand-sew. Use small neat stiches to go around the edge of each piece and then anchor by sewing a running stitch across the middle if needed (to stop the piece billowing out from the linen).

Things to Love

A Seriously Good Sofa

A really good sofa is paramount. Don't waste money on a cheapie that'll only last a few years—buy a quality sofa and it will last you 30 years. A quality sofa should be inner-sprung, constructed with a hardwood base and made locally. For longevity, select a linen-look fabric in a neutral colour that won't date—and choose a simple, classic design.

Upholstered Bedheads

For the ultimate in luxury and comfort in the bedroom, I really love oversized upholstered headboards with deep diamond buttoning. Perhaps they capture a little more dust, but they look so decadent and inviting (and it's easy enough to give them a quick vacuum now and then). If you have plain bed linen, try a subtly patterned designer fabric for the bedhead.

Curtains that Puddle

White roller blinds are functional, but boring. I would love to exchange mine for thick, full curtains that generously puddle onto the floor. I'd have linen in the living areas and silk in the bedroom. That sounds very decadent but you can find some reasonably priced linens and silks online.

Wallpapers

I love how gorgeous the contemporary versions of traditional damask-printed wallpapers are. Keep the colours light and fresh to suit a sunny climate—soft whites and pale naturals are perfect, and look especially good when finished with pure white skirtings and trims.

Fresh Flowers

Flowers can be very inexpensive, but add so much life and beauty to a home. Growing your own cut flowers would be the most rewarding, but otherwise markets sell the cheapest and freshest. Avoid generic vases though; flowers look more gorgeous in unusual vessels such as vintage jars and silver sugar bowls and teapots.

OUTDOOR ROOMS AND KITCHEN GARDENS

In your garden

It's not hard, even in the most humble home, to find a little alfresco nook you can do up gorgeously—all you need is a little time and creative inspiration. And then, to really make the most of your outdoor space, plant a simple kitchen garden and delight in the joy of growing your own food.

Vintage wicker, metal and timber outdoor furniture can all be easily found and revamped with a fresh coat of paint—just remember to use the correct primer on metal furniture. If you need new cushioning, trace the shape you require onto a piece of paper or cardboard and take your template into a foam store to have it cut. It's important to ask for outdoor foam, as regular foam will mould, even if covered in outdoor fabric.

For special occasions, I love to drag indoor furniture out—there's something so decadent about reclining on an upholstered armchair outside. You can also hang beautiful lanterns and chandeliers from a tree, or create fabric tents and scatter floor cushions on the lawn; it's the unexpected that creates an unforgettable luncheon.

Make every meal even more special by adding your own freshly picked herbs and vegies. You don't need a lot of room to start a kitchen garden—a square metre is fine—but you do need a lot of sun. To really flourish, vegetables need around six hours a day.

Sara Breckenridge, a permaculturalist who runs a kitchen garden at my daughter's school, suggests living in a new home for at least a year before planting a permanent kitchen garden—this way you get a chance to track the sun and find the best spot. In the interim, grow a few vegies in pots.

A potted kitchen garden is also a good option if you only have a balcony or small courtyard. Place the pots on castors so you can easily move the plants around to follow the sun.

Roses—the Queen of the Flowers

Roses are majestic in the garden, divine as cut flowers, and edible too.

- Ask your local nursery which varieties grow well in your region. Remember to use a good-quality soil, fertilise regularly and prune when dormant.
- Cut roses early in the morning and place immediately into cool water. Use sharp scissors for cutting and cut the stems on a slant. Keep the vase beautifully clean and top up with fresh water daily.
- Organic rose petals can be tossed into salads or sugar-coated for cake decorating.

Make your Own Compost

Making your own compost is wonderfully beneficial for your garden and for the environment in general.

In an urban environment, the cleanest and most convenient way to compost is to buy a compost bin. Place it nice and close to the kitchen to make it easier to use.

What to compost:

- Fruit and vegetable scraps
- Tea leaves and bags
- Coffee grounds
- Crushed eggshells
- Fresh lawn clippings, twigs and dead leaves
- A little shredded paper (dampen first)

A SIMPLE KITCHEN GARDEN

Once you've picked your spot (north-facing gardens are generally the best), create a raised garden bed to ensure good drainage. You can build a permanent border from sleepers, rocks or other materials; buy a pre-made raised garden bed or create one yourself by up-cycling almost any vintage container.

For example, you could drill holes into the bottom of an antique enamel baby's bath or take the bottom off a French champagne crate and place it straight on the ground. It doesn't really matter what you use as a container or border, as long as it allows plenty of drainage.

WHAT YOU NEED

Garden soil

Compost

Organic mulch (lucerne is good)

Seedlings

Trowel, fork, gloves and watering can

(all of the above supplies should be readily
   available from your local nursery)

Fertiliser (fish emulsion is good)

METHOD

1. Add soil to the garden bed. Healthy soil means healthy plants; so buy the best you can afford.

2. Mix some good-quality compost through the soil (you need about one-third compost to two-thirds soil).

3. Spread with a thin layer of organic mulch (to help keep the soil moist).

4. Plant your seedlings.

5. Water well. Feed regularly with fertiliser.

Garden Tips

- If you're placing your kitchen garden border directly onto lawn, put down a layer of damp newspaper first to suppress weed growth.
- It's important to water your garden regularly, but be careful not to over-water it. You can test whether your garden needs watering or not by poking your finger into the soil. Ideally the soil needs to be damp, not wet and not dry. It's always best to water your plants early in the morning.

- Regularly feed your plants with a little fish emulsion or other quality fertiliser

- Just a few vegies, a few herbs and a lemon tree are enough to make a substantial difference to the way you eat. If your garden isn't big enough for a lemon tree, try planting one of the dwarf varieties in a pot.

- Scatter some lavender and marigolds through your garden, they'll help repel pests and look pretty.

Five Easy-To-Grow Vegetables

Beans

Beetroot

Capsicum

Lettuce

Tomatoes

Five Easy-To-Grow Herbs

Basil

Mint

Parsley

Rosemary

Thyme

2a.

2b.

4.

after

MILKY TERRACOTTA POTS

A lived-in garden is infinitely more appealing, and one way to create the impression a garden has been around for some time is to 'age' the pots.

Terracotta pots naturally whiten with age and become beautifully covered in moss. There are ways to hasten this process with yoghurt or buttermilk, but it's a little messy and smelly, so I prefer to tone down the bright orange of new terracotta pots with milk paint instead.

WHAT YOU NEED

Terracotta pot (ensure it has drainage
   holes in the bottom)
White milk paint
Paint brush and sandpaper
Potting mix
Seedlings

METHOD

1. Paint the outside of the pot with white milk paint.

2. Lightly sand back until you get the desired effect.

3. Fill the pot three-quarters full with a good-quality potting mix.

4. Plant your seedlings.

Terracotta Tip

Terracotta is very porous, which means the pots dry out quickly and plants need to be watered much more frequently. To help retain the water, cut up an old plastic bag and line the inside sides of the pot before filling with soil. Leave the bottom unlined for drainage.

RECIPES

Herb Butter

INGREDIENTS

Parsley, oregano and any other herbs of
  your choice
Organic full-cream butter, softened

METHOD

1. Finely chop the herbs and mix them through the butter.

2. Generously spread herb butter on fresh, crusty rolls. Eat as is, or wrap the rolls in aluminium foil and bake in a moderate oven for 10–15 minutes.

TIP You might also like to try herb butter with hot corn-on-the-cob.

Pesto

INGREDIENTS

A bunch of basil or rocket (about two
   cups)

$1/3$ of a cup of macadamia nuts

$1/3$ of a cup of grated parmesan

3 cloves of garlic, roughly chopped

1 cup of extra virgin olive oil

METHOD

1. If you have a food processor, simply add all the ingredients except for the olive oil, which you drizzle in slowly with the motor running.
However, if you want to make pesto with a blender, I find you need to use more olive oil. Pour three quarters of the cup of oil in before you turn on the blender (otherwise it won't want to go at all)—then drizzle in the final quarter of the cup once the motor is running.

2. Pesto is, of course, fabulous with pasta, but it's also good on bread or as a dip. Store any leftover pesto in a jar in the fridge, and add a layer of olive oil to the top of the pesto to help preserve it.

TIP: It's more traditional to add pine nuts to pesto, but I love to use Australian macadamia nuts instead. Locally sourced nuts will also be fresher, which is quite important, as nuts tend to go rancid fairly quickly. As does olive oil, so again, choose local over imported.

Baked Baby Tomatoes

INGREDIENTS

Baby tomatoes

A few sprigs of thyme

Salt and pepper

Extra virgin olive oil

METHOD

1. Place tomatoes in a baking tray and add thyme, salt and pepper. Generously drizzle with olive oil and gently toss.

2. Bake in a moderate 180°C (350°F) oven for 10–15 minutes, or until softened.

Rocket, Pear, Walnut and Feta Salad

INGREDIENTS

A bunch of rocket

One pear, thinly sliced

A few slices of Spanish onion

A handful of walnuts

A handful of feta, cubed

A little olive oil

Juice of ½ a lemon

Salt and pepper, to taste

METHOD

1. Toss all ingredients together and drizzle with olive oil. Season with lemon and salt and pepper as desired.

Mint Tea

INGREDIENTS

One teaspoon of mint leaves

A pot of boiling water

METHOD

1. Pick mint leaves straight from your garden and let them steep for 10 minutes in a pot of boiling water. Use a strainer to pour into a teacup.

TIP: You can also try chamomile, lemongrass or ginger root. Add lemon and/or honey as desired.

Glossary

ARCHITRAVES: decorative timber mouldings around doors and window frames

BRADAWL: a small, sharp tool used to mark or make a pilot hole

COMPOST: a rich mixture of decaying organic matter used to improve soil quality

CORNICE: a protruding decorative feature joining the top of the wall to the ceiling

'CUTTING IN': a brush technique used to paint into the corners and edges of walls.

EO PARTICLEBOARD (ULTRA LOW-EMISSION PARTICLEBOARD): a more eco-friendly alternative to MDF and other particleboards. EO particleboards only contain a small amount of formaldehyde

GARDEN CLOCHE: a covered frame used to protect delicate plants and seedlings from wildlife and weather

LOW-E GLASS (LOW-EMISSIVITY GLASS): regular glass with a metal oxide coating applied, which helps to reduce heat passing through the window

MDF (MEDIUM-DENSITY FIBREBOARD): a board made primarily from wood fibres, which have been glued together under pressure and heat. MDF contains formaldehydes, so safety gear should be worn when cutting into it

MULCH: a layer of grass clippings, dried leaves or shredded prunings used to suppress weed growth and help the soil retain moisture

PELMETS: a decorative top, which hides the top of the curtain. Pelmets are usually made from timber covered in fabric

PENDANTS: any hanging light fitting

PRIMER: the first coat of paint, which is used to seal and protect the substrate

SISAL RUGS: made from the fibres extracted from the Agave plant, sisal rugs are eco-friendly and naturally dust-mite resistant

STEEL WOOL (GRADES): steel wool is graded from 0000 to 4—with 0000 being the finest and used for the likes of wax polishing and 4 being the coarsest and used for heavy duty stripping

SUBSTRATE: the surface below the finish surface, which provides support for the finish surface

TRAVERTINE: popular in Italian architecture, travertine is a form of limestone deposited by springs

UNDERCOAT: the second coat of paint. Its purpose is to stick to the primer (or existing wall paint when no primer is required) and fill any minor defects, leaving a smooth, non-porous surface for the topcoat

WOODSTOP: a water-based filler for wood, comes in a variety of colours

Acknowledgements

Firstly I'd like to thank my friend Anastasia for her stunningly beautiful photographs—and for being a joy to work with.

We'd both like to thank all the wonderful homeowners (and their families) who graciously allowed us to shoot their homes; Tess Wells, Stephen Pellegrino, Nicole Ott (and designer Nadia Aber-Griffith), Kelli Zakharoff, Janine and Geoff Tucker, Fleur Madden-Topley (and Tracy Madden), Nikki Sharp, Amber Hawkins (www.spotsandstripes.com.au), Vanessa Scoon and Kellie Armstrong (The Plantation, www.plantation.com.au)—and Marietjie Brown for inviting us in to her beautiful garden.

We're so grateful to all the tradespeople and artisans who generously shared their time and knowledge with us; Andrew Baxter from Baxter's Antique Restorations (www.baxtersantiques.com.au), who is a master craftsman and taught us so much; Jane Wilson for her friendship and sewing; Denise Kennedy from Curtain Elegance (www.curtainelegance.com.au) who selflessly shared her trade secrets with us; Steven Williams from Parry & Williams (www.parrywilliams.com.au) who expertly re-upholstered the gorgeous antique Louie love chair for us; Deborah Johnston-Booker from Johnston-Booker Faux-Finish for her painting advice, Tristan Mathieson from Austimber Floor Sanding (www.austimberfloors.com) for his flooring advice and Sara Breckenridge for her wonderful gardening advice.

It would have been hard to complete all our projects without the product support from the following companies; Porter's Paints (www.porterspaints.com); Mokum (www.mokumtextiles.com); Warwick Fabrics (www.warwick.com.au); Westbury Textiles (westburytextiles.com); Clark Rubber (www.clarkrubber.com.au) and Lincraft (www.lincraft.com.au). Thank you so much.

We'd also like to thank KT Doyle and Moore & Moore Wallpapers, Pressed Tin Metal, Livos Australia, Armadillo & Co and Moose & Bird—and all the stores who let me raid them for props; House and Doll, Twig and Grace, Just Plain Gorgeous, Coco Bloom, Industrial Revolution at The Woollangabba Antique Centre and especially Les Salles (we actually even shot the images for our original book proposal in this delicious store and have been raiding Anka ever since!).

Thanks to Patsy Rowe at New Holland, who gave me a glass of wine and believed in this book from the start—and all the girls I've worked with at New Holland, especially Diane Jardine and Jodi De Vantier.

A special thanks to my beloved father who taught me to appreciate good workmanship and the concept of quality—and to Anastasia's husband Jason who generously helped us with some of our projects—and to our little models, Saska and Scarlett Rose.

First published in Australia in 2011 by
New Holland Publishers (Australia) Pty Ltd
Sydney • Auckland • London • Cape Town

1/66 Gibbes Street, Chatswood NSW 2067 Australia
www.newholland.com.au
218 Lake Road Northcote Auckland New Zealand
86 Edgware Road London W2 2EA United Kingdom
80 McKenzie Street Cape Town 8001 South Africa

National Library of Australia Cataloguing-in-Publication entry
Scoon, Tahn.
New Vintage: The Homemade Home / by Tahn Scoon, photographs by Anastasia Kariofyllidis.
 ISBN 9781742571300
Interior decoration.
Other Authors/Contributors: Kariofyllidis, Anastasia.
747

Publisher: Diane Jardine
Publishing Manager: Lliane Clarke
Project Editor: Jodi De Vantier
Designer: Celeste Vlok
Photography: Anastasia Kariofyllidis
Production Manager: Olga Dementiev
Printer: Toppan Leefung Printing Ltd, China

Fabric credits: Page 107—Petit Trianon in Red Coral by Mokum
             Page 110—Dauphine in Dusk by Mokum
             Page 112—Icarus in Charcoal by Warwick
             Page 114, 117—Agra in Riviera by Warwick
             Page 118, 121—Edo Linen in Truffle by Mokum
             Page 130, 142—'De Rosine' in Pearl by Mokum
             Page 132-133, 158—Mica in Cigar by Mokum
             Page 138, 157—Ironwork in Ebony and Ivory by Westbury

Wallpaper Credits: Page 60—'Ticking Stripes' wallpaper by Moore & Moore
             Page 1–5, 94,127—'Flannel Flower Damask' by Moore & Moore
             Page 128—'Circus' by Catherine Martin